Yes, I'm a radical

Father Ted Colleton, C.S.Sp.

Interim Publishing Co. Ltd., Toronto

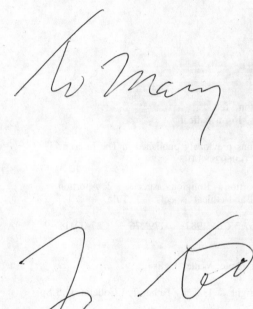

Colleton, Ted.
  Yes, I'm a radical

Columns previously published in The Interim.
ISBN 0-9692988-0-3

1. Abortion – Religious aspects.   2. Abortion –
Moral and ethical aspects.   I. Title.

HQ767.3.C64 1987   179'.76   C87-094187-9

Cover photo: Walter Uglik

Copyright © 1987 by Father Ted Colleton C.S.Sp.

1st Printing – May 1987
2nd Printing – July 1987
3rd Printing – November 1987

Published by Interim Publishing Co. Ltd.
53 Dundas Street East, Suite 306
Toronto, Ontario M5B 1C6

Dedicated To The Unborn Child

Foreword

Father Edward Colleton of the Holy Ghost or Spiritan Fathers is a prime example of why we must not give up the fight for the lives of unborn babies.

Well into his fifth year as a contributing editor and columnist for *The Interim,* Canada's pro-life, pro-family newspaper, Father Ted challenges readers to scrutinize their pro-life efforts each time they look into their mirrors.

His articles on topics ranging from abortion and euthanasia to politics and religion strike with an edge that forces the reader to an instant examination of conscience.

Father's primary interest is bringing the Good News of Jesus to those who have never heard it before. This desire led him to missionary work and a 1941 posting to Africa. Thirty years later, in 1971, Father Colleton made a personal protest to then president of Kenya, Jomo Kenyatta, on a matter of principle which broke a 'friendship' of many years standing. On being asked to retract, Fr. Ted refused and so, after three decades service as an Irish missionary in Africa, he was given twelve hours to leave his beloved Kenya. Father Colleton then became a missionary to Canada. Kenya's loss was Canada's gain.

Father Ted shoulders an exhaustive workload that stretches over fifteen hours per day, seven days per week. At an age (70±) when most people are saying,

"I've done my part, now let someone younger do the work," Father Ted sets the pace for all of us to follow.

His chaining of the gate behind the illegal Morgentaler abortuary in Toronto in 1985, catapulted him into the public eye.

His tireless efforts in defence of the unborn, his uncompromising preaching of the Good News, his infectious humour in the face of an aggressive anti-family secularism, constantly revive our spirits.

Father Ted, and other non-violent pro-lifers have been accused of being radical in their tactics to defend the unborn. Here, in his book, which contains a selection of columns which were printed in *The Interim* plus added new material, Father Ted Colleton answers those charges and proclaims: "Yes, I'm a radical."

Jim Hughes, President
Campaign Life (Canada)

Introduction

This book is not being published in response to requests from "a host of friends and admirers." This is how it all happened. A few years ago, Jim Hughes, the President of Campaign Life, phoned me. He said, "We are launching a Pro-Life paper soon. Would you write a monthly column for it?" I said, "Yes." Some thirty columns later he phoned me again and said, "We are thinking of producing your columns in book form. Have you any objection?" I said, "No."

If the book is a success, the credit goes to me. If it is a failure, please blame Jim!

Ted Colleton C.S.Sp.

Contents

viii

Respect for motherhood

People often ask me this question, "Why are you so committed to pro-life?" I consider it a compliment and hope it is true. But it is not an easy question to answer – there are so many imponderables. It's something like trying to answer the question, "Why did you become a priest?" We have to grope into the past to find an adequate reply to the many "Whys" in our lives. I shall try to find answers to the question. First of all, I was born and raised in Ireland. If there were abortions being performed in Ireland at that time – 60 to 70 years ago – it was not publicly known and was never discussed. Society would have been totally opposed to the killing of babies. Later, when studying Moral Theology, the teaching of the Roman Catholic Church was crystal clear on the humanity of the unborn child and his or her right to life.

African experience

I was ordained in 1940 and assigned to Kenya, East Africa in 1941. I worked there for some thirty years, mostly with the great Kikuyu Tribe. There are many Kikuyu customs and beliefs which would not meet with the approval of our sophisticated society – polygamy, the "circumcision" of girls, the absolute and undisputed authority of the father in the family. But one thing which always impressed the missionary was the importance of children. Every woman wanted to have children. A barren woman was considered

1

"cursed". She was an unfulfilled human being. She could be almost certain that her husband – even if he was a Christian – would "take" a second wife in order to prove that he was not the infertile one.

A logical consequence of the value in which children were held is the fact that to kill a child would have been an unpardonable offence. Women in Africa – at least forty years ago – were very definitely second class citizens. But a pregnant woman was always treated with a special respect. She carried in her womb the future of the Tribe. I am not claiming that the respect for children had a religious significance. I think it was more a natural consequence of the importance of the future of the family and the tribe. And who is to say that such an attitude does not have its roots in natural law, which ultimately is God's law for the living of human life.

Here is something which I think is significant. I can speak two African languages; one fluently, the other comfortably. But in neither of these languages do I know the word for "abortion". I never heard it in thirty years. And I didn't live in a town or city. I lived among the people out in what is called "the bush". I sat in their huts and ate their food. The Committee of Elders – corresponding to our Parish Council – was composed mainly of Christian men, who would most certainly have brought the occurrence of an abortion to the attention of "The Father". But I never heard a whisper of it.

Canadian experience

I came to Canada in 1971 – almost straight from Africa. I knew very little about Canada except that it was a great and vast country – a country flowing with metaphorical milk and honey. What was my surprise and horror on finding that in this great country the most dangerous place to be was in a mother's womb! To find that the law of the land allowed abortions supposedly for restricted reasons but, in practice, for almost any reason! To find that a doctor could set up an illegal abortuary where babies are murdered every day and it is guarded by the "Forces of Law and Order" twenty-four hours a day! All this was not just a surprise. It was a shock. I shall leave it at that. But I hope what I have written explaining the past from which I have emerged will throw some light on my actions, my words and my writings.

If the day ever comes when I shall be indifferent to the murder of 100,000 unborn babies every year, like Job I shall say "Cursed be the day on which I was born, the night when they said, 'The child is a boy.'"

3

Journey to Africa – 1941

It was suggested that I might try to brighten up this book by including a few articles on my "African Experiences". I thought I would begin with my journey to Kenya during the Second World War. It was quite an experience! I have no notes; so I am simply letting my memory dictate to the keys of the typewriter.

In 1941 I was appointed with two other young priests – both now dead – to Kenya, East Africa, as a missionary. The normal way to travel would have been to go to Southampton and take a boat bound for Kenya via the Mediterranean, the Suez Canal, the Red Sea into the Indian Ocean to Mombasa. But either Hitler or Mussolini – I can't remember which! – had his submarines blocking the Mediterranean and that changed our plans considerably.

Round the world in eighty days

On November 3rd, 1941 we left Dublin by train for Belfast; then over to Scotland by boat. After three days in Glasgow we were directed north to Oban, where we boarded a pretty miserable liner called "The Umtata". We sailed in a convoy of fourteen ships at eight knots – about the speed of a donkey and cart. The further north we went the worse the weather became. The sea was rough, the food was poor, the cabins were small and stuffy with the usual bunk beds, and the passengers were, in general, a disgruntled lot who seemed to be getting out of Britain for the duration of the war. Quite a number were young wives who were going to join their husbands in South Africa. But in the "Interim" they were quite prepared to join any willing young man after dark! Taking a walk on deck at night was a dangerous procedure as one kept tripping over prostrate bodies. After ten years in a very strict seminary, this was a somewhat rude introduction to life as it is lived in the world – and especially on board ship!

Discipline on board

The discipline on board was like being in the military forces in wartime. We had life boat drill every morning on the upper deck. Life belts – which were very cumbersome – had to be carried at all times. If an officer saw you without one you were ordered to your cabin to get it. And it was not a question of "Would you mind, sir –." but, "Go to your cabin and get your life belt or you will be reported to the captain." If one wanted to read in one's cabin at night the porthole had to be closed and the heat was stifling. To light a match or smoke a cigarette on deck at night was almost a capital offence, punishable by being put ashore at the next port. If this sounds extreme, just remember that the Atlantic Ocean was "alive" with German submarines at that time. Even the glow of a cigarette end was sufficient to invite an attack by torpedoes – and we had fourteen ships in our convoy.

Doing the wash up

Because it was wartime the staff on board had been reduced to a minimum. There were just a few waiters and the passengers had to wash up after each meal. In the seminary we had no servants and doing the wash up had always been part of the routine so we were experts. There were six priests – three from another missionary society – and we took our turns. To the amazement of the other passengers, we used to have the whole job done in record time and very efficiently. Some of the passengers strongly objected to having to do what they considered "menial work" and they complained to the mate indicating that they might refuse to do it. After all they had paid for their tickets! One evening at the end of dinner the captain's voice came over the loud-speaker, "Attention please. This is your captain speaking. I have been informed that some passengers have objected to doing the wash up after meals and even suggested that they may refuse to do it. I would like to remind them that there is a war on and this ship is under military discipline. Any passenger who dares to disobey my orders will be put ashore at the next port of call. If the Roman Catholic priests do not consider it below their dignity to do the wash up, I don't think anybody else should. Over and out." Everybody looked at our table and we weren't sure whether our popularity had risen or fallen. But there were no more complaints. The next port of call was Sierra Leone – once known as the "White Man's Grave".

A change of direction

After about a week in the North Sea we turned west and kept going until we were almost within sight of America. One day there was an alarm and we were all ordered to the top deck attired in life belts and given instructions about boarding the boats. Somebody had seen a spurt of water a few miles away and it might be a German submarine. Then there was another spurt and it was simply a whale blowing its nose. So, we all went back to doing nothing – you didn't "live" on board. You simply "existed"!

6

We then turned southeast and eventually got to Sierra Leone Harbour. There we stopped for three awful days. The heat was sweltering and there was not a breath of air. The captain and a few officers left the ship for a meeting with the captains of the thirteen other ships. But nobody else was allowed ashore. However, they were kind enough to deliver a message to the port chaplain who was also a Holy Ghost priest. He came out and spent the day with us. He also took mail to send to Ireland. This was the first time we had an opportunity to write home. Our families had no idea as to where we were or what was happening to us.

Capetown

After what seemed like a month but was in reality three days, we sailed for South Africa. We landed at Capetown nearly two months after leaving Scotland. We were allowed ashore for four hours. This was like being released from jail and we took full advantage of it. The women made for the fashion stores, the men for the pubs and the priests – also men! – for the nearest rectory. We were treated like heroes by the priests and the local bishop took us on a quick tour of the city. We gazed at Table Mountain where Cecil Rhodes used to climb when he was making his plans for his "Cape to Cairo" dream – which was never realized. We paid sad farewells to some passengers who were leaving the ship there and we sailed for Durban.

Durban

Durban is a beautiful city with a sub-tropical climate. We arrived in the harbour a few days before Christmas 1941. Then we got the "bad news". The captain announced that the ship was to return to England the next day. Most of the passengers were disembarking at Durban so they were not worried. But we three Holy Ghost Fathers had another thousand miles or so to travel to Mombasa. We spoke to the mate and asked him what we were to do. He just shrugged and said, "There's a war on and we have our instructions. What you do about it is your problem." He said he was sorry, but he didn't look it. We packed our cases, left the ship and took a cab to the Cathedral. The rector received us kindly but could not accommodate us. He got on the phone and after a few calls said we would be welcome at a hospital run by Catholic nuns. The sisters received us as if we were three of the Twelve Apostles. "Had we really braved the high seas in wartime to come to Africa to preach the Gospel? etc." We tried to look heroic but didn't feel it. Having a room to oneself after being cooped up in a small cabin with two others and bunk beds was a welcome relief.

First Christmas in Africa

On Christmas Eve, one of the local Irish priests took us to a Zulu mission outside the city for Midnight Mass. The Zulus sing beautifully and harmonize naturally. Hearing the Christmas carols sung in the Zulu language thousands of miles from Ireland brought the tears flowing down our cheeks. This was our first taste of "The Missions" and we simply lapped it up.

A great month

There was no getting out of Durban! Needless to say there was no air service. All ships leaving the harbour were full of soldiers sailing to the east, where the war with Japan was heating up. After a few days of frantic phoning and trying to get in touch with Nairobi we were advised to take it easy and relax, which we did. A Catholic Women's Society, like the CWL in Canada, heard about the "poor young Irish priests who had been cruelly cast ashore" and decided to espouse our cause. Almost every day we were taken to places of interest like "The Valley of a Thousand Hills" and we were never allowed to pay for either lunch or dinner. As priests were very few – so many were chaplains – we were always in demand to help out on weekends for confessions, Mass and preaching. On three evenings each week the Catholic Women's Society ran dances in the church hall. The main purpose was to save the young men who were pouring into Durban every day on military vessels, from the "ladies of the night" who plied a very lucrative trade all over the city. At every dance it was announced that three priests would be hearing confessions. We heard hundreds of confessions sitting on the stairs, mostly of young men who were on their way to the Eastern war zone. They knew it was their last chance of going to confession and they readily availed themselves of the opportunity. In a few days they would be the targets of the deadly Japanese torpedoes!

All good things come to an end

We were beginning to feel that we had been in Durban all our lives and might remain there. Then one morning there was a phone call which informed us that a military seaplane would be flying to Mombasa three days hence. One of the chaplains had "pulled a few strings" and got us places. We were pleased at the news but could not help feeling a little sad.

Durban had been good to us. We had made many friends among the clergy and laity and had been engaged in a very fruitful ministry. The seaplane was a real wartime effort. It seemed to be held together by bootlaces. There were no cushions on the seats – just hard wood. There were no meals and all the passengers, except ourselves, were military men. They were quite happy to sit on the floor and exchange amusing stories. It was my first experience of flying, by no means my last, but it was by far the most frightening.

Next morning we landed safely in Mombasa Harbour. Three days later I stood at a blackboard and faced my first class of African boys.

Life as a missionary in Kenya

During my ten years in the seminary, quite a number of returned missionaries were invited to speak to us about the missions. Their talks were usually interesting and inspiring. But I realized later that it is impossible to impart effectively to others what life in another country and culture is really like. Perhaps the best way – though inadequate – is to tell it as it was, without any embellishment or attempt to impress.

My first Sunday in Kenya

One of my most vivid memories is my first Sunday in an African church. It was in January 1942 – some 45 years ago! I had come from Ireland where, at that time, we seldom saw people of another colour or culture in our country. The war was on and people did not travel for study as they do today. So, entering a church packed with black faces was quite a thrill. My whole formation seemed to have been geared to this moment. Also, this was twenty years before Vatican II and in the Catholic churches of the Western world, the laity took very little active part in the Mass. They simply prayed, paid and obeyed!

Lay participation

Just as I entered the church a loud male voice intoned, "Kwa Jina la Baba..." "In the name of the Father..." The entire church took up the chant and the whole building shook as they said the morning prayer in

11

unison. They "sang" the prayers rather than "said" them and the effect on one hearing it for the first time was nothing less than overwhelming.

The homily

Father Austin Lynch – since dead – was the father in charge – or the pastor in Canadian terms. He preached the homily in eloquent Kikuyu. He had been with the tribe for ten years and was a priest of tremendous energy and zeal. What impressed me most was the attention of the people. For me the heat was overpowering, but for them it was just normal. They never took their eyes off Father Lynch. Babies howled and screamed as if there was a competition, but Father Lynch had a powerful voice and it rang through the building. Anyway, the people are so used to crying kids that they seem to be able to mentally turn off that particular area of their hearing apparatus and concentrate on what they want to hear. I think a psychologist would term it selective perception.

Have these babies no mothers?

But when the howling reached titanic proportions Father Lynch stopped for a moment. An elder stood up in the front of the church and said, "Watoto hawa hawana mama?" That meant, "Have these babies no mothers?" The effect was immediate. The mothers bared their breasts and the babies got down to business. Apart from soothing, sucking noises, silence fell on the church and the homily continued. The public breast feeding of babies in Africa is as natural as eating and drinking and does not cause either active or passive embarrassment. It took me about two days to get used to it and realize how beautiful it is.

The singing

The choir, composed mostly of school children, sang the entire Mass in Latin without looking at a book. Africans have – or perhaps I should say "had" – wonderful memories. The reason I make the distinction is this. When people cannot read or write, they have to rely on their memories. But when they learn reading and writing their memories get lazy like our own. It takes about a generation for the memories to weaken. An old man could repeat – at a land case – a speech he had heard forty years before, word for word. If he did make the odd mistake he would be corrected immediately by other elders who had also heard the speech.

The social aspect of Sunday

Unlike the impersonal climate of our city churches, church going in Africa was both a religious and a social event – as it is in country parishes all the world over. After Mass the Africans do not rush home. They stand around and talk and laugh. The women compare babies and clothes, the men discuss local court cases and the weather, the older boys and girls eye each other with interest and the children play with sticks and stones. I found it fascinating how African children could entertain themselves. There were no radios or TVs or phonographs. Neither were there hockey sticks or tennis racquets. One football could engage forty African boys for hours. The younger children made balls out of banana leaves just as we used to out of paper. They invented their own games. I don't think I ever saw an African girl with a doll. But from the age of five they were looking after their baby brothers and sisters. There was never a shortage of babies – and what are dolls but substitutes for babies!

The parish council

Since Vatican II most parishes in Europe and North America have a parish council. But it was not always so. In the Missions, however, every parish had a Council of Elders known as the Kiama cha Wazee. "Kiama" means a council and "Wazee" means elders. It would be very imprudent for a priest to attempt to run a parish on his own in Africa as they used to do in Ireland... you had to remember that almost every family at that time was divided between Catholics and Protestants and pagans. Most of the men were still pagans and they were the single authority in the compound. So the entire family programme had to be taken into account. Masses had to be scheduled at times that would not interfere with the milking of the cows and the goats or the gathering of the harvest. Often the Mass times had to be changed to suit the seasons. All this had to be discussed at the council meeting. The priest usually attended the meetings but he was never the chairman. The latter was elected every year and was usually a man of prominence who was respected in the community. There was always something to discuss and arguments could be very heated. It was a very democratic society and every opinion had to be listened to and voted on. If a priest could not get on with the Council of Elders, he usually had to leave the mission for the whole tribe would be against him. Like Irish families, they might fight among themselves but they would unite against a common "enemy".

A special day

Although the majority of the Kikuyu Tribe were still pagan, Sunday had become a special day all over. The Christian Missions had been in Kenya about sixty years when I arrived there and had made quite a social as well as a religious impact on the people. Sunday was a day to attend church if you were a Christian or for taking it easy if you weren't. It was a day for dressing up and going on walks and playing games. What about "dating"? Well, Africans, like young people all over the world are very "sex conscious". There are plenty of "illegitimate" children. But there was one cultural taboo which came as a surprise. It was this. Any display of affection in public was totally forbidden by the custom of the tribe. What happened in the bushes was a private affair. But what happened in the market place was a tribal affair. Coming from a "Christian" part of the world and particularly after my journey on shipboard where almost anything was acceptable, even in broad daylight, it was a surprise and a relief to find these people who were considered "pagan" so conservative about public behaviour. It made me wonder why we had come! They were particularly strict on the girls. If a girl, even in her twenties, was seen kissing a man in public she would be sure to get a good beating from her father – who would most certainly hear about it. The beating was administered – where nature intended! – with a whip made of hippo hide. It was called a "Kiboko". The British Government forbade the use of it in jails and schools as it was too severe. But they never dared interfere with family discipline. So, the kiboko was considered the ideal instrument for beating the bottoms of naughty girls – it made a lasting impression! If a young wife became too "flighty" at the market, she could expect an even larger dose of the kiboko if her husband heard about it.

Common sense

At first I could not understand all this. After all, "purity" was considered a Christian virtue but, even

in 1942, sexual permissiveness was becoming the accepted mode of behaviour in Europe and North
America. So, how come such strictness in a pagan
country? Some of the older priests explained to me
that the Africans considered this a matter of common
sense. They didn't have to read the Gospel to know
that sex is like fire. As long as it is controlled and
disciplined it can do wonderful things for society and
the family. But when it becomes a "towering inferno"
as it has today, it can wreak untold havoc on society
and the family. Africans are extremely "family conscious". The women are considered the heart and guardian of the family. Conseqently any sign of "loose-
ness" was unacceptable in a woman – a future mother.
Needless to say the ideal was not always attained, but
the principle stood.

What about the men?

An obvious question usually asked by women and
girls is this. Could the men and boys get away with
anything? Africa was – and I think still is – a "man's
world". Women's Lib as we know it in North America
would not have lasted half an hour in the 1940s.
Justice was very definitely "lopsided". But there was
one crime that was totally outlawed and that was rape.
A man found guilty of rape was publicly flogged –
which is done in some Arab countries today. The
reason was again related to the family. Motherhood
was held in the highest respect, and to make a moc-
kery of it – as rape does – could not be tolerated.
You may not agree with the punishments – and I'm
not sure that I did – but the whole matter is worth
thinking deeply about. There is a great deal of common sense about the attitude of what we might dub
"the primitive mind" regarding the social importance

of keeping the power of sex within the limits dictated by nature – that is within marriage. In fact, it is probably true to say that the survival of a Christian society will depend on the extent to which sex can be tamed again. We may have a lot to learn from those whom we presume to teach!

Would the real Dr. Mengele please stand up

When I was at college, I didn't major in history – I majored mostly in meals! But I do love to dabble in history, both ancient and modern and there is a great deal to be learned from just reading history. Wasn't it the philosopher, George Santayana, who said, "Those who do not learn from the mistakes of history are doomed to repeat them" – or words to that effect?

When the rumour started recently that the notorious Nazi doctor, Mengele, was still alive, the world was shocked – I hope – by the mind-chilling stories of his diabolical experiments on helpless human beings in the death camps of Germany. And we lay all the blame on Hitler and his gang of Nazi criminals. We cringe at the idea that certain human beings, who were termed *untermenchen* or 'less than fully human', were experimented on and then discarded as garbage – all in the interests of a more pure human race.

Eugenics

Eugenics is the science which concerns itself with the betterment of the human race through improving heredity. The word itself was coined by an English scientist named Francis Galton, who was a cousin to Charles Darwin. The science of inherited physical characteristics was pioneered by the Austrian monk, Mendel (1822-1884) – don't mix him up with Mengele – but it was Galton who speculated as to whether characteristics of behaviour were inherited. Bad behaviour as well as good.

Sterilize the unfit

These theories of 'heredity' gave birth to the 'eugenic campaigners' who wanted a human race made up of 'thoroughbreds'. And, like Mendel's plants, they had to be carefully cultivated. From this philosophy, sprang the idea of getting rid of those of 'inferior breed'. That is, all those who showed signs of feeble-mindedness, alcoholism, criminal tendencies, waywardness (a euphemism for promiscuity), pauperism (being poor) and, in general, all those with undesirable or anti-social manifestations. But how was the creation of this 'super race' to be achieved? It was very simple. By government decree, all the 'unfit' were to be sterilized to prevent them from breeding their kind and so 'staining' the race.

The first eugenicists

The Eugenic Societies came into existence between the 1890s and the 1930s – long before Hitler. They had the support of some of the most respected names in England and America. Sidney Webb, founder of the London School of Economics and *The New Statesman*, was one of the leaders. So were scientists like Sir Julian Huxley (older brother of Aldous of *Brave New World* fame) and J.B.S. Haldane. The feminists got into the act in a big way under the leadership of Margaret Sanger (America) and Marie Stopes (Britain). Sex expert, Havelock Ellis, and writer, George Bernard Shaw, plus inventor, Alexander Graham Bell, were strong advocates of the campaign to 'clean up' the human race. Theodore Roosevelt and Winston Churchill are said to have been 'sympathetic' to the

19

movement. The eugenicists had several obsessions but their main fear was that the 'lower orders' would outbreed the 'superior classes' and their solution was the sterilization of those whom the State declared to be 'unfit'. That they were not fully successful in their efforts is obvious by the fact that you and I are still around!

Green with envy

When Hitler came along and promulgated the 'eugenic sterilization' law which forcibly sterilized the feeble-minded, schizophrenics, epileptics, the blind and all those who suffered deformities (which were 'offensive' to the perfect society), some American eugenicists were green with envy. One of them wrote, "The Germans have beaten us at our own game."

It's still happening

Have we learned from the mistakes of history? Not at all. In fact, great 'progress' has been made in the manner of the selection of the 'unfit'. These days, one doesn't have to be feeble-minded or schizophrenic in order to qualify for extinction. You just have to be 'inconvenient' or 'unwanted' or 'conceived out of due time'. It's really easy to pass the 'unfit' examination. You don't even have to go to the trouble of being born. Big Brother is watching you even while you are in your mother's womb, and if you don't measure up to certain specifications, decided by your mother or the doctor or society in general, one of two things will happen to you. The first is that you will simply be crushed or vacuumed out of existence. The second is that you may have the honour of being experimented on – while you are still alive – for the good of the human race.

Outlandish?

If this seems outlandish, go back to the September issue of *The Interim* where you will read the following. "In Britain, experimentation on dead aborted babies and on 'spare' embryos" – still living – "has been going on for some time. Publicity on these experiments followed the blocking of a private member's bill that would have prevented experiments on embryos." The British government-appointed Warnock Commission Report recommends that experimentation on embryos be allowed up to fourteen days after conception. Do you think they will stop there?

I believe Hitler is dead. But I'm not sure about Doctor Mengele.

We never thought it would go that far

What has become known to history as the "Nuremburg Trial" began on November 20th, 1945. An indictment was lodged against twenty-four former Nazi leaders, charging them with numerous crimes against peace, conventional war crimes, crimes against humanity. The chief crime was the killing of millions of innocent human beings, not only Jews (the largest number) but also gypsies (the most exterminated group), Slavs, political prisoners and undesirable civilians – this included the handicapped (physical and mental), the old and anybody who came under the heading of what Hitler dubbed, "useless eaters". In a word, those who failed the "Quality of Life" test!

Who carried out these killings? They were not what we would term "madmen" in the ordinary sense of the word. No, in general they were normal, average, bourgeois, working class, professional, men and women who had been brainwashed by a totally materialistic philosophy. Neither was this mass killing a disorderly orgy of primitive violence, but a mass action lasting for years and carried out with pedantic orderliness.

Perhaps the most interesting moment in the trial, at least for those of us who are pro-life, was seen when the Nazi defendants were asked if they had anything to say in their defence. One of them stood up and said, "Your Honour, we never thought it would go that far". United States Justice Robert H. Jackson replied, "It went that far the first time you condemned an innocent human being to death". That is the foundation of the Pro-Life Movement. The right to life of every innocent human being – born or unborn. Once we decide to play God and condemn any innocent human being to death, everybody becomes vulnerable. After the war some German doctors looked back in horror on the Hitler regime and were genuinely puzzled. They asked themselves, "How did it all begin?". It began before Hitler came to power. The German psychiatrists had paved the way for the Führer. In 1931 a group of Bavarian psychiatrists advocated the sterilization of the chronically mentally ill. This step was followed by an insidious corrosion of medical thinking and, logically, of medical ethics. If we can sterilize persons without their consent, we have relegated them to the status of animals. One downward step leads to another and soon the doctors were deciding who should live and who should die and so on down the "Slippery Slope".

Could anything like this happen in Canada? Not only could it happen but it has happened and is happening every day in our midst. Doctors sit on the "Throne of God" and sign the death warrants of those who are not considered fit to be born because they may cause embarrassment and inconvenience to their families and friends.

God grant that the day may come soon when Canadian doctors will look back on the horror story of nearly one million Canadian babies killed in ten years and not only ask themselves, "How did it all begin?" but follow it with the more important question, "When is it going to end?".

The man who stood alone

His name was Franz Jaeggerstaetter but you will not
find it in any 'Who's Who' in the world. He was
what would be called 'a small Austrian farmer' with
a wife and two young children and when Hitler united
Austria to Germany by force in the 'Anschluss' of
March 1938 he was probably in his early thirties.
Franz had only grade school education but he was a
man of high intelligence and strict moral principles.
He had read and heard the speeches of the Führer;
he had studied the Nazi philosophy and he found it
impossible to reconcile that philosophy with his Christian convictions. He had come to a very definite decision. Nazism was an immoral code; Hitler was an
immoral man; Franz Jaeggerstaetter would never submit to Hitler or his henchmen.

From the time Hitler entered Austria in triumph in
1938, Franz made no secret of his opposition to the
Nazi regime. (When hail destroyed the crops in the
area, including his own, the Government – in order
to gain favour with the people – provided disaster
relief. Franz refused to accept handouts from the
Nazis.) Up to 1943 his open contempt for the Nazis
was not considered serious as it was confined to his
own friends in his native village. (He was popular
with the villagers and did not have any enemies.) But
in February 1943 everything changed drastically.

An edict was issued that every able-bodied man
must join Hitler's army. When his turn came to be

24

registered in the army, Franz simply said, "No, I won't join." His friends asked him why. He replied, "My conscience will not allow me." He was advised to talk to his parish priest and the priest explained the difference – in moral theology – between 'formal' and 'material' cooperation in evil. He told Franz that it would not be wrong to join Hitler's army as he did not intend to do evil and the consequences if he refused – execution – were so dire that he would morally be excused for doing so.

Franz prayed about it and thought about it but his conscience remained the same. He would not join. It was the function of the men of the village council to implement the order to join the army and they told Franz if he joined they would put him in the Medical Corps, so that he would not have to do any killing, but simply look after the wounded. He made his position very clear. "If I put on the Nazi uniform I would be pretending to agree with Hitler and his policies. I don't, so it would be a lie in action."

They got a lawyer to try to convince him of his foolishness. The lawyer asked him, "Franz, has any German or Austrian bishop in a pastoral letter called on Catholics to refuse to join the army or support the war?" "Not that I know of," responded Franz. "And there are millions of other German and Austrian Catholics who are joining up with no problem of conscience, so what makes you so different?" Franz's answer was again simple and uncomplicated. He said, "I guess they don't have the grace to see it as I do, but I do have the grace and my conscience tells me I cannot join."

Franz Jaeggerstaetter was executed as a traitor on August 9, 1943 – a solitary witness to truth!

All this seems so very far away from us both in time and space that we might see very little practical connection between the problem which Franz faced and any personal situation of our own. But let's make a few changes in the actors, the details and the year. It is 1983, and you are a builder or an electrician or an engineer. Your company gives you the job of working on a new clinic. When you have studied the plans and asked a few questions, you find that it is to be an abortion clinic. What would you do? To refuse to cooperate would mean losing your job. A moral theologian would probably advise you that, under the circumstances, you could go ahead and build this house of death. After all, you are not going to perform any abortions. And of course you would never do such a thing! But just building the clinic in which others will deal out death to unborn babies, well, that's different – or is it? If you could call Franz on the phone, what would his answer be?

We could apply the same principle to countless situations germane to the abortion issue – don't compromise with evil even on the periphery! I think it is the Ojibwa Indians who have this wonderful saying in their folklore, "Cowards walk in crowds; the brave in single file." Think about it!

Stop the world,
I want to get off

Oh boy! Dull moments around here are about as plentiful as white blackbirds.

I returned from Europe to find *The Interim* office buzzing with questions, counter-questions and speculations regarding the morality of using vaccine extracted from an aborted baby to innoculate school children against rubella.

According to reports, the vaccine being used in Canada was extracted from a Swedish aborted baby in 1962. The research was performed at Stanford University in California. From the cells of this one baby literally millions of cells have been multiplied, to the extent that the whole world could be innoculated with this particular vaccine. All this is mind-boggling but it does not answer the question, "Is it moral to use this vaccine to innoculate the children?"

Heart versus head

My initial reaction to the whole business was one of repulsion and disgust and it still is. But is the action immoral? My heart cries out, "Yes, of course it is."

But my head calls a halt and says, "Cool it. Did you not study the principles of moral theology? Well, just apply them coolly to the case in point." Reaching back over nearly half a century and applying the principles of proximate and remote co-operation in an immoral act, I have to – reluctantly – admit that I cannot say that either injecting the vaccine or receiving it is, in itself, an immoral act. As I write this, I can almost feel my heart turning somersaults. But, truth is truth.

Some distinctions

Having said that, there are some important distinctions to be made. Of course the action of aborting the baby was immoral in the first place. Whether it was done 20 years ago or 20 minutes ago does not enter into the morality of the question. The time factor is about as relevant as the nationality of the baby. If you asked me if it is moral to abort a baby in order to obtain the vaccine, my reply would have to be a very positive negative. An abortion is always immoral no matter how good the intention may be. If the baby was not alive when the cells were extracted, I still have strong objections which I hope to show later in this article.

So, to recap, the abortion was immoral. The act of using the vaccine by someone who had nothing to do with the abortion is not, in my opinion, immoral in itself. But, we just can't leave it at that because there are too many far-reaching implications.

Fetal research

What is medically and scientifically termed, 'fetal research' is a very dangerous and slippery slope descending to unsounded and unsearchable depths.

It is in this area that I see the gravest objection to any use of human embryos that would lessen the dignity and sanctity of the human person. Perhaps I can best explain what I mean by giving a few examples of things which have occurred in recent years but which are not generally known to the public.

TV sets, soft drinks and cookies

In 1976, Dr. Sophie Perry, Director of the Department of Pathology at the District of Columbia General Hospital, revealed to the press that the staff had collected more than $68,000 from commercial firms for organs of stillborn and premature babies. The money was used to buy a television set for the lounge and to cover expenses for soft drinks and cookies for visiting doctors.

Beauty products

In April 1981, guards at the Swiss-French border intercepted a truck load of frozen fetuses destined for French cosmetic laboratories. This was reported in the *Gazette du palais*, a reputable legal journal, which explained there was a busy trade for fetal remains for "beauty products used for rejuvenating the skin, sold in France at high prices".

Pesticides

In 1977 the Environmental Protection Agency in the U.S. acknowledged that an Ohio medical research company tested the brains, hearts and other organs of nearly 100 fetuses as part of a pesticide research project.

Live babies exploited

An anesthetist, giving sworn evidence before an abortion commission in Pennsylvania said, "It was repulsive to watch live fetuses being packed in ice while still moving and trying to breathe, then being rushed to the laboratory."

The *World Medical News* reported in June 1973 that Dr. Peter Adam of Western University had performed an experiment at the University of Helsinki, Finland. He cut off the heads of live babies, delivered by Caesarean section. He then ATTACHED THE HEADS TO A MACHINE which pumped various chemicals through the brain circulation of the severed heads. *The American Journal of Obstetrics and Gynecology* reported in January 1974 that live, beating hearts of preborn babies up to 15 weeks old were removed for experimentation at the University of Szeged, in Hungary.

The Nuremberg Code on Human Experimentation

After the Nuremberg Trials the world was horrified at the evidence produced showing the uses to which human bodies had been put by German doctors in research laboratories. An international code was drawn up, known as 'The Nuremberg Code on Human Experimentation'. Here is an extract: "For research to be ethical, the subject must give consent. The person is violated if unwillingly – even uncomprehendingly – he/she is used for the benefit of others."

Even assuming that parents can give consent for minors, would anybody believe that parents had signed a consent form for the bodies or organs of their offspring to be used as pesticides or beauty products? Would any mother consent that the head be cut off her living baby so that a doctor could try some new experiment?

Perhaps there are mothers who would agree to this for some consideration. But I sincerely hope and pray that there are not!

What does all this mean?

The accumulation of all these facts, which have been documented, adds up to only one fact. Science has lost its sense of morality. Scientists – not all of them, of course – have lost sight of the trees in their preoccupation with the wood. But the 'wood' in this case is composed of individual 'trees' each made in the image and likeness of God and possessed of the inalienable right not to be exploited in the interests of any other being – human or otherwise.

If society is prepared to sit comfortably on its hands and accept the exploitation of human beings which I have listed above, I feel like shouting, "STOP THE WORLD, I WANT TO GET OFF!"

31

Are legal and moral
the same thing?

The Globe and Mail on May 21, 1983 reported from Regina that 'anti-abortionist' Joe Borowski was "astounded" that the federal government lawyer did not call witnesses to counter his (Joe's) legal attempt to have Canada's abortion law declared invalid. Mr. Borowski's lawyer, Dr. Morris Shumiatcher, had produced a number of world experts in genetics and fetology who left any unbiased reader of the reports in no doubt as to the humanity of the fetus from the instant of conception. Yet, the federal lawyer, Edward Sojonky, said that these arguments were not relevant to the issue at stake. The only important thing to be settled is whether Section 251 of the Criminal Code, dealing with therapeutic abortions, is valid.

In other words, if Section 251 can be proven valid according to legal arguments, it doesn't matter a jot if human beings are being killed. One has to admit that, from Mr. Sojonky's point of view, the 'legal' issue is all that he is being asked to prove. But from the 'human' point of view the argument is ominous. If the law says you may kill, you may kill.

That same issue of *The Globe and Mail* reported that Albert Helmut Rauca had been extradited to Germany to stand trial for killing Jewish Lithuanians during the War. According to Mr. Sojonky's logic, if Mr. Rauca's lawyer can prove that what he did was legal at the time, then Mr. Rauca should be declared innocent – no matter how many people he executed. It was legal because it had the force of the law back up his actions.

Here is the wording of a letter written by Adolf Hitler in October 1939. It was predated 'September 1st' so as to save the doctors who had 'jumped the gun'. "Reichleader Bouhler and Dr. Med. Brant are responsibly commissioned to extend the authority of physicians, to be designated by name, so that a mercy death may be granted to patients who according to human judgement are incurably ill according to the most critical evaluation of the state of their disease." The letter is signed Adolf Hitler and is written on his own private paper. This letter did not give an order to kill but it gave power to kill 'legally' and the doctors took full advantage of it, as history records.

Professor Robert Havemann denounced the 'euthanasia' murders with these words "...the patient is no longer a human being needing help but merely an object whose value is measured according to whether his life or his destruction is more expedient for the nation. The physicians took over the function of judge over life and death – they made themselves infallible gods."

Does this sound familiar?

Could this happen in Canada?

In 1977 the Badgley Committee (set up to study the implementation of our abortion law), reported that it could. Many physicians, whom they met on their visits to hospitals, "...openly acknowledged that their diagnoses for mental health were given for the purposes of expediency and they could not be considered as a valid assessment of an abortion patient's state of mental health." (p. 212)

33

In other words, the doctors 'openly admitted' that they had taken over the decision of life and death as a matter of expediency. I can't see any difference, in principle, between this statement and that of Dr. Havemann quoted above.

Dr. Christoph Hufeland (1762-1836) was a 19th century physician who had a vision of things to come. He stated: "If the physican presumes to take into consideration in his work whether a life has value or not, the consequences are boundless and the physician becomes the most dangerous man in the state."

Ontario doctors
betray their calling

"The thoughts of youth are long, long thoughts." I can't remember who wrote those words but they are part of a poem I learned in school more than sixty years ago. I recalled them recently when reading a historical novel by Ken Follett entitled *Wings of Eagles*. It is the story of the rescue of two American businessmen who had been imprisoned in Iran without trial, around the time of the famous American hostage crisis.

Loyalty

The president of the company, Ross Perot, is determined that he will not desert his two friends and employees. Having tried every legitimate means, and having received very little co-operation from people in high places in the U.S. government, he decides, at tremendous risk, to organize a rescue team. Sitting alone in his Dallas home, his mind goes back to his father, who was a man of great loyalty to his friends, irrespective of their colour or social position. Follett writes, "Another of his father's principles was, 'Take care of the people who work for you.' Ross could remember the whole family driving twelve miles on Sundays to visit an old black man who 'had used' to mow their lawn, just to make sure he was well and had enough to eat." Ross was about twelve at the time and he is now in his sixties. But he knew that it was the example of his father's loyalty that inspired

35

him "not to count the cost" in his efforts to free his friends from their plight.

The things we forget

If you are still with me, you may be wondering where all this is leading. Well I am writing at the height of the doctors' strike and when I read the above quoted sentence my memory skipped backwards over something like sixty-seven years. I saw a small boy (myself) looking out the window of an Irish farmhouse and watching a man on a bicycle coming through the gate. As we say in Ireland, "The Heavens had opened and the rain was falling in bucketfuls." The man with the bicycle was the local 'country doctor'. He had cycled some seven miles in the rain to visit my young sister, who had a fever. I was about six at the time but somehow the drenched figure burned into my mind this conviction, "A doctor is somebody who will do everything possible – even at great personal sacrifice – to be with his patients when they need him." Of course I could not have formulated it like that. But that is what it meant to the receptive mind of a child.

Through the years

And that assessment of the doctor as a man of duty has travelled with me through the years. As a priest in Africa I always worked closely with the doctors in the 'bush' hospitals and I can never remember one – over a period of thirty years – who 'let the side down'. I can see, even now, a young English doctor – with no religion – standing in the burning sun at 2 p.m. every day while an endless queue of Africans came one by one to voice their physical ills. An African nurse translated them into English. He couldn't learn the language but his patience never wavered as he

36

treated each one as if he or she was the only person in the world. He used to laughingly say to me, "I'll look after their bodies, Father, and you can look after their souls." In fact, without realizing it, he looked after both! If there could be such a thing as a 'secular' priest, that was my definition of the doctor.

A fallen idol

But this ideal of the doctor as 'a man apart' in the natural sphere, as a priest is 'a man apart' in the spiritual sphere, now lies in pieces at my feet. It was not because the doctors went on strike. They probably had a just cause. I am not competent to judge. No, it happened one evening while I was watching the news on television. The picture showed a hall full of doctors – representing the medical profession of Ontario – applauding loudly when it was announced by the chairman that emergency wards in several hospitals would be closed down on the following day. Something died inside me! The only comparison I could think of would be an official body of priests applauding the announcement that dying Catholics would be refused the Last Rites of the Church. In other words, the betrayal of a vocation!

Proportion

We all have rights and we have a right to defend our rights. But there is such a concept as 'proportion'. If the neighbours infringe on our rights by making a hole in the adjoining fence or by allowing their dog to trespass or by parking their car in our driveway, there are certain ways in which we can react. But we will not – I hope – shoot their dog, burn down their house, smash their car or beat up their kids. Such actions would be out of proportion to the undoubted wrongs they have inflicted on us.

37

I believe there were various methods the doctors could have employed in order to express their strong disapproval of Bill 94. They could have made things very inconvenient for the government and the public without endangering the health and the lives of their fellow human beings. Their heartless action has left a scar on the face of a noble profession – a scar that will still be visible when the children of today become the parents of tomorrow. "The thoughts of youth are long, long thoughts!"

How did the psychiatrists get into the act?

When we read that, according to official statistics, 95% of all abortions in the Western world are performed on alleged 'psychiatric grounds', it would seem legitimate to ask, "How did the psychiatrists get into the act?" This is especially so when the distinguished British psychiatrist, Dr. Myre Sim, M.D., F.R.C.P., F.R.C., PSYCH., D.P.M., states in relation to this figure, "There must be something wrong here. Either there is a new psychiatric disease which has been met by every other psychiatrist except myself – or there is some big fiddle going on." (1980)

An interesting horse

The story of how the psychiatrists got into the act is sad but interesting, and should be a warning to society. Up to 1938, the law in England forbade abortions, except when the physical life of the mother was at stake. But in 1938 a tragic and significant event took place, which radically changed the social outlook on abortion in England and eventually throughout the Western world.

As *The Times* of London related the story, some teenage girls were chatting with the guards outside a barracks. One of the guardsmen told them that in the stable, round at the back, there was a famous horse which had a wooden leg and a green tail. He invited them to come and see this interesting animal. Only one girl, aged fourteen, agreed to go to the stable.

She was raped, not only by the guard who had invited her, but by three others. She became pregnant – the only recorded case of pregnancy resulting from rape in the medical literature of England up to that time.

Misplaced compassion

In England at that time, there was a distinguished gynecologist named Dr. Alec Bourne. He was a man of compassion and integrity who for a long time had felt that the legal grounds for abortion should be widened to include those women who suffered psychologically from unwanted pregnancies. He was a member of the Abortion Law Reform Society.

The girl was referred to him and he took a bold step. He considered this a classic case, and laid his professional life on the line. He performed an abortion and then informed the police. He was charged before the law. As far as I know, the penalty at that time was life imprisonment.

Enter the psychiatrist

A well-known psychiatrist, the late Dr. J.R. Reese, agreed to give evidence in favour of his friend, Dr. Bourne. His argument was that, if the girl had been forced to carry the pregnancy to term, she would have suffered a severe mental breakdown owing to post-partum psychosis. Up to that time, Dr. Reese had never treated a patient for post-partum psychosis.

The judge, knowing that Dr. Bourne was a distinguished and respected member of the medical profession, did not wish to send him to prison. So, in summing up, he said that the fact that the law did make an exception – the physical life of the mother – meant that it was not watertight. There could be other circumstances. Turning to the jury he said, "Today, I think, we have found one of these circumstances."

The doctor was acquitted and, although England remained conservative on the abortion question until after the war, the thin edge of the psychiatric wedge had found a chink in the law. The opinion of a psychiatrist in good standing regarding the possible mental effects on the mother became a convenient and imponderable handle on which to argue almost any abortion case.

The floodgates are opened

In 1967, after a number of unsuccessful attempts, the Abortion Act was passed in the British Parliament and the floodgates were thrown entirely open to what has become virtually abortion on demand in England. The last figure I remember for England was 150,000 in one year, not counting the thousands who come from other countries to have abortions at the expense of British taxpayers.

Sorry, too late

But there is a very interesting conclusion to the story. In 1967, Dr. Alec Bourne, then 81 years of age, opposed the passing of the Abortion Bill. Here is his statement, "If this law is passed it will open the gates wide for 'phoney psychiatrists' and 'phoney gynecologists'." He resigned from the Abortion Law Reform Society and became a member of the Society for the Protection of the Unborn Child. It is said – I have it only on hearsay – that he suffered awful pangs of conscience because of the part he had played in bringing about easy abortion.

Somebody has said, "Compassion without principle

is extremely dangerous." And it certainly is. Dr. Bourne was not an unprincipled man, but he allowed his compassion to blind him to the principle of the sanctity and inviolability of every human life. Seeing the dreadful effects of what he had done and realizing what the future could hold, he regretted his action of thirty years before and did what he could to redress it.

Money v. morals

In 1963 a very well-known British psychiatrist wrote a paper for the *British Medical Journal*. In it he stated that, on the grounds of evidence he had collected over thirty years, he could find no psychiatric justification for abortion. Some of his London collegues accused him of "taking the bread out of their mouths". The then President of the Royal Psychological Association said to him, "You are absolutely right, but you have taken away all our room for manoeuvre." How many more thousands of babies will be sacrificed before society wakes up to the fact of what is really happening?

The oath of medical ethics

"If the physician presumes to take into consideration in his work whether a life has value or not, the consequences are boundless and the physician becomes the most dangerous man in the state."

The above statement was not made in 1983 by the president of Right to Life or by a Roman Catholic bishop. It was made by a German physician named Dr. Christoph Hufeland, who lived from 1762 to 1836. If I had read it twenty-five years ago, I would have considered it exaggerated or at least irrelevant to the medical and social situation in our time. But I would have been wrong!

Let me say first that I have a tremendous respect for the 'science' of medicine and also for the many wonderful doctors whom I number among my friends, and into whose capable, skilful and moral hands I would have no hesitation in placing at least the physical portion of my person. But, having paid this sincere tribute to individuals, I have to confess that I entertain grave fears regarding the well-being of some areas of the medical profession. To take one example among many, a report in the Toronto *Star* of April 4th, 1983, must give cause for some concern.

A survey of 300 Toronto doctors reveals that two-thirds of them (200) have neither taken the oath forbidding mercy killing nor read the Canadian Medical Association's Code of Ethics.

Among those who did take the Hippocratic Oath, two-thirds don't remember what it says, and three-fifths (180) of those questioned say that nothing would be lost if the Oath was no longer taken.

I don't know how you feel, but that admission makes me very uneasy, especially in view of recent medical experiments and developments in Canada and the United States.

If doctors are so hazy about the Hippocratic Oath and what it stands for, I do not think it would be out of place to say something about Hippocrates and his famous Oath.

Hippocrates was a Greek physician who lived during the 5th and 4th centuries before Christ. He was referred to in ancient times as 'Hippocrates the Great' and Aristotle in his *Politics* speaks of him as 'The Great Physician'. Although he died about 370 B.C., he was called, at least until recently, the 'Father of Modern Medicine'. The reason this man who lived some 25 centuries ago held such an exalted position in the minds and hearts of the members of the medical profession irrespective of their race, culture or religion, was that the Oath which bears his name was the foundation of medical morals and ethics for more than two thousand years. And though Hippocrates himself may not have actually formulated it, until very recent times, it was an honoured custom for every doctor to take this Oath – and keep it!

What was the wording of the Oath? It is rather long and involved, so I shall quote only the salient points. It says,

"I swear by Apollo and all the gods and goddesses that, according to my ability and judgement, I shall keep this Oath and stipulation... I will follow that treatment which, according to my ability and judgement I consider best for the benefit of my patients and abstain from whatever is deleterious and mischievous. I will give no deadly medicine to anyone if asked or suggest any such counsel. Furthermore I will not give to any woman any instrument (pessary) to produce abortion. With purity and holiness I will pass my life and practice my art."

We have evidence that, at least until 1948, this Oath remained the abiding principle upon which the art of medicine was founded. Its values were enshrined in the Declaration of Geneva by the World Medical Association in September 1948. It says in part, "I will maintain the utmost respect for human life *from the time of conception.* Even under threat, I will not use my medical knowledge contrary to the laws of humanity. And I make these promises solemnly, freely and upon my honour." It is very significant that this Oath, made by a pagan doctor to a pagan god, should have been accepted as the basic ethic of medicine as practised by Christian doctors in a society which, at least in theory, had accepted the principles of the Gospel. Not only was it accepted as the standard of Christian medicine but as the standard of good medicine all over the civilized world.

So, even by pagan standards, the *raison d'être* of the doctor's vocation was, from the very beginning, to care and cure but never to kill. It is a sad commentary on the present state of medical morals that it can be statistically proven that the most dangerous place to be today is in the womb of a mother!

Infanticide

The word 'infanticide' comes from two Latin words, 'infans' (an infant) and 'caedere' (to kill). So, 'infanticide' is 'killing an infant'.

Up to a few years ago I was under the false impression that infanticide was a very unusual occurrence especially in 'civilized' places – just as, up to a dozen years ago, I thought that abortion was a very exceptional happening. Then I read the following statement by Dr. C.E. Koop, at present Surgeon General for the United States. He said, "Well, you all know that infanticide is being practised right now in this country (U.S.A.) and I guess the thing that saddens me most is that it is being practised by the segment of our profession which has always stood in the role of advocate for the lives of children." I decided to do some research on infanticide in the United States.

As night follows day

What might be termed an 'epidemic of infanticide' followed the 1973 Supreme Court decision, which declared that an unborn baby is not a human person and therefore does not have any rights – not even the right to be allowed to live. Law is one thing; logic and reason another, it seems.

If a doctor is permitted by law to kill a baby before it is born, what is to stop him from killing it after it is born? Every doctor – with one sad exception –

46

knows that a baby in its mother's womb is a human being. Therefore, why quibble over the small question of time and place?

So if a baby, not wanted by its parents, is by an 'unfortunate' accident born alive during an abortion procedure, what do you do with it? Why not just kill it? If you allow it to survive you will incur the anger of the parents and the embarrassment of having 'botched' a simple operation! The police are not looking in the windows and the staff is on your side from the start.

The quality of life

That is one aspect of the subject. Another is the question of the newborn baby who appears to be a poor prospect for attaining 'meaningful humanhood'. After all, doesn't society need full-blooded, healthy, intelligent human beings like ourselves? So why allow these lesser human breeds to survive and become a drag on society and a burden on the tax payer? It's all very simple and logical and you shouldn't have the cops looking over your shoulder in the operating room.

Does this really happen in the most sophisticated country in the world? Yes, it does! After the Supreme Court abortion decision of 1973, 43 babies were 'allowed to die' at Yale New Haven Hospital intensive care nursery. Vital treatment was deliberately withheld. (*Newsweek*, Nov. 1973)

Thousands of babies

According to the *Stanford Law Review* February 1978, "Every year thousands of parents decide to withhold or withdraw medical treatment needed to keep their severely defective newborns alive." Yet, as far as the

47

general public is concerned, this – unlike abortion –
is largely a hidden practice. But, now and then, there
is publicity and a court case follows. I have space to
relate only one such case, but it should be sufficient
to indicate what is happening to society.

The Waddill case

In 1977 Dr. William Waddill performed a saline abortion on a seven-month fetus. But the injection did not
'take' and the baby girl was delivered alive. The doctor
panicked and called in a pediatrician, Dr. Cornelsen.
After the incident, Dr. Cornelsen could not live with
his conscience and he reported what had happened to
the police. Dr. Waddill was charged with murder.
During the first trial, Dr. Cornelsen told the jury that
he had seen Dr. Waddill attempt three times to strangle
the baby. He finally succeeded in the fourth attempt.
There was also evidence from the autopsy that the
baby had died from strangulation.

The first trial resulted in a hung jury and the judge
declared a mistrial. In the second trial, by a majority
of eleven to one, the charges against the doctor were
dismissed. After the second trial the one juror who
held out for a guilty verdict told reporters that the
other jurors discounted the evidence given on the principle that the baby was already dead because the
mother wanted it dead!

An abortionist doctor has been quoted as saying,
"If you agree to do an abortion, you can't present a
woman with a live infant. It is a breach of contract."
So, if the baby is born alive by mistake – you just
strangle it.

What has happened to
the human race?

Dr. Eugene Diamond, professor of pediatrics at the Stritch School of Medicine in the U.S. sums it up thus, "American physicians have been the instruments responsible for the deaths of millions of aborted babies. Now, putting aside the curettes and salt syringes – our profession lifts its eyes above the windows of the abortorium and gazes into the nursery." That gaze is cool, professional, speculative and sinister. With social acceptance of infanticide – and it's just round the corner – it envisages a new way to dispose of an old problem – the congenitally-deformed child. The life of the baby is weighed in the balance against parental hardship, financial burden, general family welfare and its own chances of attaining the 'quality of life' desired by modern society. And guess who loses!

Everything has happened before. Here is a quote from the book, *Whatever Happened to the Human Race?* by Francis Schaeffer and C. Everett Koop. It is in reference to what happened in Germany when Hitler attained the pinnacle of power. "The first to be killed were the aged, the infirm, the senile, the mentally retarded and defective children. Eventually, when World War II approached, the doomed undesirables included epileptics, World War I amputees, children with badly modelled ears and even bed wetters. Physicians took part in this planning on matters of life and death to save society's money." (p.106)

Could it happen in Canada?

I believe it is happening but has not yet come to light. But it has got to come because infanticide

follows abortion as night follows day! In *Judgement at Nuremberg* one of the condemned Germans said, "We didn't think it would go that far." The American judge replied, "It went that far the first time you condemned an innocent human being to death."

Thou shalt not kill

Infanticide is not a horror coming upon us in 1984. It has been here for some time – in the United States, in England, in Canada and around the world. According to the *Globe and Mail* last June, a doctor, who admits he deliberately ordered an overdose for an infant girl in Edmonton's University Hospital, said, "Euthanasia is happening everywhere but nobody is talking about it."

He was referring to the widespread custom of allowing handicapped babies to starve to death. The doctor, whose name is Dr. Nachum Gal, told the *Edmonton Journal*, "Silence imposed on doctors by doctors is the way of society."

Can this be really true – that doctors take it upon themselves to starve human beings to death or murder them with overdoses of lethal drugs? Not only can it be true, it is true.

Is Hitler really dead?

At a conference on 'Infanticide and the Handicapped Newborn' held in the U.S. a few years ago, Dr. Eugene Diamond, Professor of Pediatrics at Loyola University of Chicago's School of Medicine made some shocking revelations.

Among other things, he told the 420 delegates from around the world of the results from a conference

51

entitled 'Ethics of Newborn Intensive Care'. The assembled doctors were asked this question, "Would it ever be right to intervene directly to kill a *self-sustaining infant*?" The 20 doctors replied as follows: 17 said "Yes" (i.e., it would be right to kill a child); 2 said "No". One was "uncertain". So 85% of the specially-selected delegates take exactly the same position as did the doctors in Nazi Germany before the war.

Here is a quote from a book called *The German Euthanasia Programme* by Frederic Wertham (1978): "A further method of child euthanasia was deliberately and literally starving children to death. In most instances these deaths were recorded as normal or natural deaths."

The book quotes from Ludwig Lehner (later a public school teacher) who visited a children's hospital in Eglfing-Harr in 1939: "In the children's ward were some twenty-five half-starved children ranging in age from one to five years. The director, Dr. Pfanmueller, explained the routine, 'We don't do it with poisons or injections. Our method is much simpler and natural.' With these words the fat and smiling doctor lifted an emaciated, whimpering child from his bed, like a dead rabbit. He went on to explain that food is not withdrawn all at once, but rations are gradually decreased. 'With this child,' he said, 'it will take another two or three days.'"

What price a child?

Dr. Diamond went on to discuss what he termed, "A Dorian Grey-like deterioration among professionals concerned with newborns." One of the arguments for killing disabled children is that it costs too much to care for them. Dr. Diamond, to take one class, the mentally retarded, noted that children with Down's

Syndrome do far better at home than in an institution.

He went on to say that it costs about $12,000 per bed per year to institutionalize a child. About 5,000 children are born with Down's Syndrome in the U.S. each year. To keep them in institutions would cost one-tenth the amount of money spent per year on dog food.

Britain more 'advanced'

According to Dr. Everett Koop, Surgeon General for the United States, infanticide is perpetrated even more frequently in Britain than in America. The child's parents are led to believe that when a child is born with spina bifida, either an operation is performed and the child gets well or an operation is not performed and the child dies. This is not the case.

Spina bifida is not a lethal illness. But it is now the custom in Britain to operate only on the less-deformed children. Doctors joke about putting the other babies on a 'LOW CALORIE DIET', WHICH REALLY MEANS STARVING THEM TO DEATH. This is known as 'a process of selection'. Another euphemism for murder.

We will not be muzzled

According to Dr. Gal, "Euthanasia is happening everywhere but nobody is talking about it." We do intend to talk about this abominable crime against our children.

We hope you do too.

Hysterotomy

Murder by any other name –
is Murder

Semantically speaking, we are living in an age of
'Euphemism', smoothing the rough edges of distasteful facts. For instance, there are no old people these
days, there are only 'senior citizens'. We don't die
any more, we just 'pass on'.

Murder

Murder is defined as 'the unlawful and premeditated
killing of one human being by another'. But murder
is often dressed in euphemistic titles which make it
sound less heinous than it really is. One of these is
the medical title, 'hysterotomy'.

What is hysterotomy?

The word 'hysterotomy' is derived from two Greek
words, 'hystera' meaning 'uterus' and 'tomia' which
means 'incision'. So, etymologically speaking, Caesarean section is a hysterotomy, but, medically and morally speaking, there is a world of difference between
the two. The difference is that between life and death.

The implications

Implied in the term 'Caesarean section' is the clear
understanding that both mother and baby are to be
saved. But when the term 'hysterotomy' is applied to

what is almost identically the same procedure, the implication is that the mother is to live. The baby is to die.

Human sensibility

For a person who is fully pro-life, all abortions are equally wrong in principle because an innocent human being is done to death. Civilized people would consider all murders, no matter how committed, to be equally wrong in principle. But, from the point of view of human sensibility, there is a difference between killing a person by a painless lethal injection while they are asleep and bashing their head in or flaying them alive.

Different abortion procedures

There are several abortion procedures, all of which are horrible. From the point of view of human sensibility, I think, hysterotomy is the most shocking and inhuman. I shall give my reasons as concisely as possible.

Hysterotomy is used only when a baby has passed the fourteenth week of gestation. The reason is that after the fourteenth week the bones are more firm and rigid and other methods would be dangerous and more traumatic for the mother.

Get ready

Now get ready for the horrendous aspect of hysterotomy. The fact that an abortion is put under the heading of hysterotomy means that the baby was removed, whole and entire and alive from its mother's womb! Here is a quote from a book entitled, *Rites of Life* coauthored by Landrum Shettles, M.D., and David Rorvik:

"Hysterotomy is nothing other than Caesarean Section. We call it 'hysterotomy' when we want to kill the child, 'Caesarean' if we want to save it. In either case a live baby is likely to emerge. If it is to die, then it must die of neglect."

"All of these babies move, breathe, and some will even cry. One will live a few minutes, others a few hours; the more advanced ones can survive for days. If the baby has reached twenty-two weeks gestation, it could survive if cared for. After twenty-six weeks, survival – in cases of Caesarean Section – is commonplace. At thirty-six weeks, chances of survival are 100%"

Starved to death

But when the procedure is classed 'hysterotomy', the baby is simply left to die of neglect. You might ask, "But does this really happen in Canada?" The answer is, "YES". Here are the proofs.

According to Statistics Canada, in the years 1980, '81 and '82, 129 hysterotomies were performed in Ontario. Of these, 64 were performed in Toronto hospitals, and Sunnybrook Hospital alone accounted for 20. Is this murder? If you can find a nice euphemistic term for it, let me know, because I can't. In my opinion, not only is it murder but, in the words of Shakespeare, it is "Murder most foul".

Johnny

During July, 1984, I spent a very enjoyable month as chaplain to the Nazareth Catholic Family Life Centre. It is run by Don and Posey McPhee at Combermere near Barry's Bay in Ontario. Parents with young families come here from different parts of Canada, the United States, and even Australia to spend a week's vacation – as a family – in a very relaxed, informal and Christian atmosphere. Don and Posey and their five children set the pace and a staff of 20 young people, some of them volunteers, do the chores (including baby-sitting) and leave the parents free to swim or boat or just browse and read.

Johnny

I first saw Johnny from my bedroom window just after I had arrived. A young man and three boys were throwing a ball to each other out on the lawn. One of the boys seemed to be sitting down but when the ball was thrown to him he dragged himself along the ground after it, picked it up and threw it back. I realized that he was severely handicapped and my first reaction was one of pity. Poor kid! What a life!

Next morning, I met Johnny at breakfast. He was sitting in his wheelchair at the end of the table and beaming at everybody. He couldn't wait to get breakfast over to go out and play baseball with his dad, his two brothers and a few friends. Later, I saw him swimming in the lake. As the week wore on it became

57

obvious to everybody that the one thing you didn't do to Johnny was pity him.

He loved exchanging jokes and wisecracks with everybody. Of a group of lively, noisy and adventurous kids, Johnny was the star. It was not because he was handicapped but because he has a scintillating and attractive personality. He really enjoys life to the full.

His parents

I asked his parents if we could have a private chat, as I wanted to know more about this ten-year-old boy who seemed to thrive on what would normally be considered an insurmountable handicap. Jim and Mary Reid, both in their early thirties, were delighted to talk about Johnny. The story is as follows.

After a few years they had one child, Christopher. They lost their second child before birth, and Mary was told that she could not have any more, so they applied to be foster parents.

After a year, they received a phone call telling them that there was a baby boy available, but that he suffered from spina bifida. They went to the home and were introduced to Johnny, who was then two months old. His natural father just didn't want him and his mother, although she would have accepted him, was not strong enough to oppose her husband.

Rejected

So, Johnny was rejected by his natural parents. The Reids did not hesitate for a moment. They accepted him as if he were their own, and they told me with tears in their eyes (and there were a few in mine) that they considered him a tremendous blessing from God. Mary said, "If his parents only knew what they gave up!" A short time after this, Mary became pregnant again, and now they have a younger boy. She is expecting her third child in October.

Love

I asked them how the other children related to Johnny. They said, "He's just one of us. In fact he is the centre of the family. He both gives and receives love." After eighteen months of fostering, Johnny was to be 'put up for adoption'. The Reids immediately applied to have him, and their request was granted.

School

How does he do at school? Johnny is an 'A' student and is very popular with his school-mates. He is an ardent fan of the Blue Jays, and never misses a game if he can help it. He is very proud of some pictures of himself shaking hands with some of the Blue Jays stars.

There's nothing wrong with me!

An amusing incident occurred when Johnny was about six years old. A friend of the family who was in the Charismatic movement kept insisting that they should take Johnny to a healing ceremony in the hope that he would be cured. Mary was not too keen, but she agreed, to please her friend.

As they were slowly moving up the aisle for the blessing Johnny asked, "Where are we going Mom?" Mary explained as best as she could and said, "You might be cured." Johnny said, "Cured of what? There's nothing wrong with me!" So he returned home, 'uncured'.

A terrible thought

One day, as I watched Johnny playing and laughing with his friends, a really terrible thought occurred to me. What if Johnny's mother had been subjected to amniocentesis? Given their attitude, his natural parents would almost certainly have aborted! Jim and Mary would have been deprived of this 'tremendous blessing' and the world would have been denied another ray of sunshine.

The more I meet the Johnnys of this world, the more convinced I become of this fact. There is no such thing as an 'unwanted child'; there are only 'unwanting parents'.

God so loved the world...

After a long and learned lecture on love, a parishioner said to a priest, "Father, don't lecture us on love – just love us!" I suppose people expect to hear a lot about love from the pulpit and it has been a favourite preaching topic for centuries. But it is interesting to find that – in quite recent years – the psychologists and psychiatrists have discovered that genuine love, expressed in a human way, is probably the best – and in some cases the only – effective treatment for emotional and even for physical illness.

Karl Menninger

Here are a few of the multitude of statements from eminent people in the world of medicine. Dr. Karl Menninger of the Menninger Clinic in Kansas, U.S.A., writes that, "Love is the medicine for the sickness of the world." He told his staff, including doctors, nurses, orderlies and cleaning people, that the most important thing they can offer the patients is love. He says that when people learn to give and receive love they recover from most of their illnesses whether physical or emotional.

The inability to love

According to Eric Fromm, psychologist and social philosopher, loneliness and the inability to love are the underlying causes of psychic and emotional disorders. And the famous Swiss physician and writer,

Paul Tournier believes that people need to remove their masks and discover and be discovered by other people. He says that simple love and honest friendship can bring healing.

The barrier between conscious self and other people

The professor of clinical psychology at the University of Illinois is Dr. Hobart Mowrer. In his opinion, emotional illness results from a barrier between the conscious self and other people, "It is our inability to love and be loved, to have friends and be a friend in any depth that causes much contemporary illness. When honesty and sharing of life begin, healing often follows."

Carl Rogers

Everybody who has even dabbled in psychology or counselling has at least heard of Carl Rogers, founder of the famous 'nondirective' School of Counselling and author of many books including 'Client Centred Therapy'. He says that he can quickly train for counselling those who have what he, apologetically, terms 'love'. He says there is no other word for this quality which makes a good counsellor. He adds that, without love no amount of training can make a man or woman a good counsellor.

God so loved the world –

Is this a new discovery? By no means. "Long time ago in Bethlehem –" the world was given a lesson in love which has never been equalled. It took the experts in human psychology 2000 years to arrive at a rediscovery of this lesson. Christ could have come into this world in any way He wished. He could have been a king or a president or one possessed of limitless wealth and power. Instead He chose to come in the form of a helpless Babe who had nothing to give but LOVE! The early Christian writer, Tertullian (2nd Century) described the Child in the Crib as "Omnipotence in bonds". The image of God in swaddling clothes has gripped the attention of the world in every age and in every clime and will continue to do so as long as the world needs love. And if ever the day comes when the world does not need love – there won't be any more world!

Pictures that tell stories

I think that everyone who 'puts pen to paper' or 'mouth to mike' has written or said something about the Pope in the past few weeks surrounding his visit to Canada. Most have been laudatory while some have been pejorative. If there had been no criticisms of some of the Pope's statements, I would have been concerned, for it would have meant one of two things – either he had said nothing worthwhile or people had not been listening! After all, the Man whose Vicar he is, was crucified for the things He said.

The handicapped

Like most people I was impressed by the pageantry, the enthusiasm of the crowds and the amazing stamina of the Pope himself. But more than all else I was deeply touched by the 'person to person' attitude of the Holy Father in his meeting with people. Where I first noticed this was during his visit to the home for the handicapped in Quebec. One of the handicapped – a very handicapped man – read an address of welcome. The Pope sat and listened with utmost attention. His eyes never left the man's face. It appeared that he was hearing things he had never heard before. Later, as he walked among the handicapped he spoke to each one personally and each one was for him 'the most important person in the world' for that moment. When one considers the tremendous burden of office that weighs on his shoulders, this is a truly remarkable quality in a world which tends to value people in the measure of their pragmatic use to society, and in a man whose subjects are clustered in every corner of the globe.

The children

The expression which seemed to appear in almost every article about the Pope – even in those which were critical of his teachings – was the word 'sincerity'. If the Holy Father wears a 'mask', as psychologists tell us we all do, it is the most transparent mask I have ever seen. Crystal clear sincerity seems to shine from his person. Sincerity is a quality which defies description but which can be recognized by the simple, the unlettered and especially by children. Not only did the Pope reach out to the children but the children reached out to the Pope. Children are naturally fearful of adults. It is one of their built-in securities. But, children of all sizes, shapes and ages responded to the Holy Father in a way which seemed to echo the words of the Gospel, "Let the children come to Me – for such is the Kingdom of Heaven."

The Pope at prayer

In my opinion, the most impressive moments of the entire Papal pilgrimage were those when the Holy Father knelt in prayer! He seemed, in those brief seconds of solitude, to be entirely absorbed in God. Just as his smile, the lifting of his eyes or the raising of his hands could bring a crowd to life, so, the bowed head, the closed eyes, the clasped hands created an atmosphere of reverence which pervaded the souls and minds of prelates, priests and people. This was no 'performance' for the sake of giving a good example to priests and people. It was a 'person to person' communion with his Lord. Watching him in those so intimate moments I felt that I had all the answers to all the questions which surround the exceptional personality who is John Paul the Second. Hundreds of Canadians have written about the Pope – bishops, priests, sisters and lay people. But, for me, the one who summed up the Holy Father in the fewest but most trenchant words was Barbara Amiel in her article in the Toronto *Sun*. She described him thus, "The complete Man of God." And Barbara is Jewish. Thank you Barbara!

On the rock of ages

While the Pope was travelling in Western Europe, I was travelling in Western Canada – the security was not quite as tight! I was moving even faster than the Holy Father and so I could follow his 'progress' in different local newspapers.

The style of reporting was, of course, a little varied but there was one common denominator – the use of such adjectives as 'conservative', 'traditionalist', 'unyielding', etc. And, of course, the word 'Polish' was often added – as if to suggest that a pope of another more up-to-date nationality (Canadian or American, for instance) would bow to the pressures of modern society and declare that the 'traditionalist', 'conservative', 'unyielding' teaching of the Catholic Church on basic moral questions was now obsolete and would be changed officially as soon as the Pope got back to Rome.

On the rock of ages

But, of all the articles I read on the Pope's tour of the Netherlands, I think an editorial in *The Globe and Mail* (May 16) was the most spineless, unprincipled and illogical. It also completely lacked a sense of history. Under the title of "On the rock of ages", the writer seemed to be saying that, while there are really no eternal verities – all is change, revolution, upheaval, etc. – it would be nice if there were a few anchors to hold on to. But there are none and the

67

Pope should change the teaching of his Church which is based on century-old traditions.

To quote just one example, the editorialist states, "The Pope maintained that the Church's opposition to promiscuity, homosexuality, birth control and abortion is fixed forever, and forever is a very long time." What the writer is really saying is that morality should be decided by vote.

Down the slippery slope

Let's take one example from history. In 1908, the Lambeth Conference of the Bishops of the Church of England denounced "the use of all artificial means of restrictions of the family". In 1930, the Conference declared that, "where there is a clearly felt moral obligation to limit or avoid parenthood – the primary and obvious method is complete abstinence from intercourse". But if there was morally-sound reasoning for avoiding abstinence, "the Conference agrees that other methods may be used, provided that this is done in the light of Christian principles".

At the Conference of 1958, a resolution was passed, stating that the responsibility for the number of children was laid on the conscience of the parents. Ten years later, in 1968, the Conference considered a papal encyclical, *Humanae Vitae*, and disagreed with the Pope (Paul VI).

In 1973, the Board of Social Responsibility of the Church of England supported the Humanist campaign for a free family planning service for all, irrespective of marital status and regardless of age.

The following year, in 1974, the British Department of Health issued a memorandum of guidance to doctors. This states, "Parents of a child are not to be contacted – regarding the provision of contraceptives – without the child's permission."

I mention these facts of recent history to show what happens when there is no strong voice to defend traditional morals. The Church of England had obviously kept in step with the deteriorating morals of English society and had voted accordingly. That is far from spiritual leadership!

An excellent letter

In reply to the sad editorial to which I have referred, a gentleman named David H. Martin wrote a letter to *The Globe and Mail* which succinctly summed up the situation.

Here is what the *Globe* printed (May 27) in their Letters to the Editor column. "If the Church, in her first centuries, had followed your prescription for institutional success – consulting opinion polls and striving anxiously to read the sociological currents of the times, instead of humbly following her Master, she would not have confronted the Roman world but adapted to it and would today, no doubt, be a footnote in history, a strange sect known only to antiquarians."

Man's search for meaning

The Viennese psychiatrist, Victor Frankel, survivor of a Nazi concentration camp and author of the much-read book, *Man's Search for Meaning*, once observed that "Man has an infinite capacity for deceiving himself". He/she sure has!

And that is why the world needs a John Paul II, who has the courage and tenacity to withstand the winds and waves of the secular humanistic society in which we live, move and have our being. We need

this man of rock-like quality who, when all the verbal
brickbats have bounced off him, can stand before the
"ranting of the mindless mob" (a quote from *The
Globe and Mail*) and calmly but firmly restate the
traditional position of his Church on basic morals:
This is the way it has been; this is the way it is; this
is the way it will be. Long may he reign!

What is a practising Catholic?

I am writing this in January 1986. It was announced on the radio this morning that Maureen McTeer, a 'practising Roman Catholic' and wife of Joe Clark, has agreed to become an honorary director of CARAL. The announcement went on to say something to the effect that, while Ms. McTeer would not have an abortion herself, she supports the right of any woman to have one as she supports the right of a woman to control her fertility.

I don't think it is necessary for me to say that I totally disagree with Maureen's action and position but that is not what I wish to write about here. I would prefer to dwell on the media's constant use of the term, 'practising Roman Catholic' as applied to people like Maureen who, either by their actions or their words, take a public stand against the official teaching of the Church.

The media has not the 'foggiest' notion about the meaning of being a Catholic. For instance, when the Pope was celebrating Mass at Downsview, a commentator said, "Mr. John Turner, a devout Roman Catholic, receives Communion from the hands of the Pontiff." Very touching! But I have heard Mr. Turner at least three times speaking with obvious pride about his part in piloting the present Abortion Law through Parliament in 1969. That law has been mainly responsible for the murder of well over 1,000,000 Canadian babies. If John Turner is a 'devout' Catholic, I'd hate to meet a 'non-devout' one after dark.

I don't like the expression 'practising' and 'devout' as applied to Catholics, or members of any other religion for that matter. They are imponderables. I would much prefer the term, 'true Catholic'. The expression is Cardinal Newman's. It does not mean that he or she slavishly accepts everything the Pope or a bishop or a priest says. But it does mean that they accept the official teaching of the Church in matters of faith and morals.

Official teaching

The Catholic Church's official teaching on abortion is crystal clear. Vatican II referred to abortion as an unspeakable crime *(The Church Today)*. The present Pope never allows any opportunity to pass in any part of the world, without strongly condemning the killing of the unborn. But abortion is not wrong just for Catholics because the Church says it is wrong. The Church teaches that abortion is immoral because abortion is immoral, and would be immoral even if Christ had never come on earth. It is interesting that abortion was first forbidden by the Law of Hammurabi 1700 years before Christ. The fact that Maureen McTeer is a Catholic is not relevant. So why do the media frequently add the tidbit 'a practising Catholic' when they announce such aberrations as Maureen McTeer's latest?

When the media use the term 'practising Catholic' I wonder, what do they mean? I have a suspicion that, for them, being a practising Catholic equals attending Mass on Sundays. I remember a country parish in Ireland where a big dog used to sit quietly at his master's feet all during Mass. The hound was physi-

72

cally present but he would scarcely have been rated a 'practising Catholic'. He didn't even contribute to the collection! But by media standards he would be a practising Catholic because he was physically present in the Church on Sundays.

'Catholic' politicians

There must be hundreds of 'Catholic' politicians in North America who are about as Catholic in their thinking as Colonel Kaddafi. They bow to Christ on Sundays and vote with Caesar on Mondays. One of the best-remembered sayings of Christ is this, "Render to Caesar the things that are Caesar's and to God the things that are God's." But we must not render to Caesar the things that are God's. And human life, born or unborn, belongs to God.

And so, all those 'Catholic' politicians like John Turner, Maureen McTeer – a politician not *per se* but *per alium* – Ted Kennedy and Geraldine Ferraro are only fooling themselves and trying to fool others when they claim they are Catholics.

The statement attributed by the media to Maureen McTeer – that, while she would not have an abortion herself, she supports the right of any other woman to have one – sounds very tolerant and compassionate. But it is exactly the same as saying, "I wouldn't commit murder myself but I support the right of any man to kill his mother-in-law if she's interfering with his way of life. After all, every man has a right to his own particular type of lifestyle."

My advice

If an act is immoral in itself, no person who claims to be moral can support or condone it. They may feel

73

compassion for the person who has, under stress, performed the immoral act. That is very different from supporting or condoning it.

So, for the benefit of the mixed-up media, my advice to John Turner and Maureen McTeer and 'Catholics' of similar ilk is this. Be logical. Either be a public Catholic or leave the Church. But don't try to march to the beat of two drums which move in opposite directions. The God who rules the Church on Sundays and the Parliament on Mondays is one and the same God. There is only one God. And He beats only one drum!

I am pro-choice!

During the Mother's Day Rally and Walk for Life in Toronto on Sunday May 8th, 1983 the pro-abortionists had a plane circling overhead with a streamer tied to its tail. The banner read, "Motherhood by choice: not by force". It looked beautiful against the bits of blue in the sky and as I watched it I found myself agreeing with both statements. Of course motherhood should be by choice and never by force. No woman should be forced to marry and outside marriage she has neither the right nor the obligation to perform the act by which a child is conceived. If she is married, she is still free to choose, provided she does not contravene the rights of somebody else.

Not a unilateral decision

How could choosing not to be a mother infringe upon the rights of another? When two people marry, they have equal rights regarding the big decisions of their partnership. Surely the question of whether or not to have children is not a minor issue! So a wife, who, against the wishes of her husband, refuses to have a child, is denying her husband the right to be a father. She is not being faithful to her contract and covenant.

Already a mother

Another way in which a woman can infringe upon the rights of another is by refusing to continue a pregnancy. She is not refusing to be a mother – she

75

already is one by the fact that she has conceived. She is, in fact, terminating her motherhood along with the life of her child. She has a physical choice, just as a man with a gun has the physical choice to blow somebody's head off. But, like the man with the gun, she has no moral choice because nobody has the right to kill another human being. There is no geneticist or fetologist of any standing today who would deny that each human life is in existence from the moment of its conception.

The rallying cry

The slogan 'Freedom of Choice' has become the rallying cry of the pro-abortionists. It has had much success because unthinking people do not follow the expression to its logical conclusion.

Freedom to do what? The answer is 'freedom to kill a child'. Nobody is free to choose to take a life for whatever reason. Freedom of choice ends where the rights of others begin, and the right of the unborn to live begins at the moment of conception. So the statement, "I am pro-choice" is morally valid when seen in its proper context.

Our choices are always limited

If your choice is a personal one which does not contravene the rights of another or the laws of God, then you are free to choose. But, if your choice infringes on the rights of others or on the commandments of God, you are NOT FREE. Abortion not only breaks the commandment of God, "Thou shalt not kill", it also tramples on the basic right to life of an innocent human being. When a human life is at stake, it is not pro-choice – it is no choice!

If we could only phone Solomon

There is nothing quite so convincing as a good slogan if it is repeated often enough. Isn't that the principle on which most of our advertising is based? The slogan doesn't have to be true to be effective – a half-truth will do quite well.

Half-truth

A typical example of the 'half-truth' slogan is the pro-abortion cry, "Every woman has a right to control her own body." Of course every woman has a right to control her own body but within limits. Legally, no one of us has an absolute right over his or her body.

The laws of society do not allow us to mutilate our bodies or to abuse them by taking drugs. People who have consumed too much alcohol are not allowed to drive a car. Just try 'streaking' down University Avenue at noon and you will find that the police will take control of your body!

Definition of a woman

According to Webster's dictionary, 'woman' is defined as 'a female human being'. Since over half of the babies who are aborted are female human beings, it is obvious that the pro-abortionists are not being honest when they say "Every woman, etc." The female human being in her mother's womb who is aborted is certainly not given any choice as to what happens to her body.

But isn't the fetus part of the mother's body?

The theory that the fetus is part of the mother and does not have a distinct life of its own is so outmoded that one feels pedantic in even mentioning it. But it is still being used in defence of abortion, so we can't overlook it.

Every year at the Right to Life Rally we are treated to the scream of "Not the Church, not the State; women will decide their fate." We are quite prepared to go along with this statement as long as it does not mean the killing of another human being – which abortion does mean. But just get an earful of this one.

At a rally of women in Rome in 1976 in support of abortion on demand, the following declaration was made: "The body is not to be managed by the doctor and even less by God. The womb is mine and I can manage it myself." If you can't believe it, write to the *Philadelphia Enquirer* which reported it on April 4, 1976 (page 4C).

They keep missing the point

In the question of abortion, we are not talking about the woman's body but the baby's. So, speaking about the mother's right over her own body is missing the point. Scientifically speaking – and that means genetics and fetology – there is no doubt about the fact that the child in its mother's womb is a distinct, unique human being and not part of the mother.

Common sense

Even without the assistance of fetologists, ordinary common sense should convince any one with eyes to see and ears to hear that the fetus is distinct from its mother. Surely a male fetus is male before it is born.

Can a body be male and female at the same time? Many women carry children who have a different blood type and factor from their own. We know that it is impossible for one body to have two different blood types.

Whose baby?

But probably the most devastating argument against the nonsensical theory that the baby is part of the mother is the report (*Los Angeles Times*, June 22nd) that a team of physicians at Harbor-UCLA has successfully transferred an embryo from one woman to another. Whose baby is this? Quick, phone Solomon!

The unlearned lessons
of history

Here is a quotation from *The Story of Civilization* (Volume 3) by the famous historian, Will Durant. It is taken from Chapter three which is entitled, "Why Rome Fell".

"In Greece the depopulation had been going on for centuries. In Alexandria, which had boasted of its numbers, Dionysius calculated that the population had, in his time, (250 A.D.) been halved. He mourned to see the human race diminishing and constantly wasting away. Only barbarians and orientals were increasing – outside the Empire and within. What caused this fall in population? Above all, family limitation. Practised first by the educated classes, it had now seeped down to the proletariat, famed for its fertility; by A.D. 100 it had reached the agricultural classes, as shown by the use of the imperial 'alimenta' (hand outs) to encourage rural parentage. By the Third Century it had overrun the western provinces and was lowering manpower in Gaul. Though branded as a crime, infanticide flourished as poverty grew. Sexual excesses had reduced human fertility."

He ends the chapter with this sentence, "Rome was conquered, not by barbarian invasion from without but by barbarian multiplication from within."

Could it happen again?

In the *Sunday Star* of March 16, Richard Gwyn wrote a very arresting article under the title, "Low birth rate clouds West German future". According to Gwyn, West Germany is suffering from a mental disease called, 'kinderfeindlichkeit' which means, 'dislike of children'.

He says, "In all affluent, western societies, the birth rate has dropped below 'replacement' rate of 2.2 children to each family. Canada's birth rate is 1.7. As a consequence, our population is growing more slowly and is aging." He says that West Germany's condition is an entire order of magnitude more acute. "It is, literally, a dying nation."

Today, West Germany's population is 62 million. By the year 2050 the number of Germans could decline to 38 million. At present the birth rate is 1.4 children per family – the lowest in the world and the lowest in recorded history. Gwyn quotes University of Cologne sociologist, Peter Scheuch, as saying, "The change came in the 1960s, with the celebration of the importance of individual self-realization. Children are now seen as an obstacle to the fulfilment of personal career and leisure aspirations."

Sounds like the German edition of the 'Me Generation'. Almost half (47 per cent) of German children are growing up without any brothers or sisters.

Children unpopular

"It's an adult world in Germany to which children have to adapt," says Heinrich Sudmann of the Ministry of Youth, Family and Health, "Here children are regarded as a nuisance..." Richard Gwyn goes on to say, "In restaurants in West Germany couples with children are greeted with frowns, while those with dogs in tow are greeted with smiles. Few hotels have spare beds or cots for couples travelling with children."

The armed forces

The Government is getting worried about the falling birth rate. One reason is the difficulty of keeping up the armed forces. In order to maintain the army at the committed level of 500,000, West Germany has extended the term of conscripts from 15 to 18 months and is debating whether to open combat positions to women. In 1985 there were 117,000 too few eighteen-year-old boys to serve in the forces! But, in spite of the 'writing on the wall', the abortion mills are thriving. According to Richard Gwyn, "There are an incredible 300,000 abortions in Germany per year – incredible when compared with 600,000 live births." He continues, "But, for an entire society to apparently accept its shrinkage passively, as seems to be happening in West Germany, is something quite else."

According to official statistics, in 1985 there were 113,000 more coffins than cradles. Just try a similar working system with your bank account and see how well-off you will be in a few years!

Not confined to West Germany

But this 'depopulization' is not confined to West Germany. Holland with a population of some 13 million, has emptied 3,300 classrooms in ten years. France's population has so diminished that they are depending on Moslems from their former colonies to keep up the work force. The Moslems – not being Christians! – do not believe in birth control, so they have large families.

Dr. Emmanuel Tremblay, a French scientist, has calculated that – if things continue as now – France, once the 'eldest daughter of the Church' will be predominantly a Mohammedan country by the year 2035. That is 55 years from now. In 1571 the Mohammedan Turks were prevented from invading Europe by their defeat by the Christian forces in the Battle of Lepanto.

How much worse...

Today, out of 21 million 'guest workers' in Western Europe, some seven million are Moslems. On average, Moslems have three times the number of children Christians have. The prophet Mohammed urged his followers to conquer the world with the "sword in one hand and the Koran in the other." A modern saying among Moslem leaders is this, "We don't need the sword any more – we have the children!"

When somebody sympathized with Helen Keller on her physical blindness she replied, "How much worse it is to have eyes and refuse to see."

Population implosion

We have heard and read so much recently about nuclear war, the arms race, acid rain and the inevitability of ecological disaster, that it is a relief to wake up in the morning and find that the world is still with us! I do not wish to deny that these are all serious dangers but I am not so sure about their inevitability. To take just one – nuclear war. Somewhere in the back of my head (or perhaps in the depth of my soul), there is a feeling that Almighty God is not going to allow some political nut to press a button which will wipe out His world and everything in it.

The real problem

If we are voting on what is the biggest problem facing the world today, my vote goes to population. Not the population 'explosion' but the population 'implosion.'

Here are a few demographic facts which should arrest our attention. It takes an average of 2.2 children per woman to replace the population of any country over time, excluding immigration. This is obvious. If John and Mary have two children, they are just replacing themselves – provided the two children live to adulthood. But countless children die in infancy and childhood, so we need the 'point two' of a baby extra to make up for the losses.

A grim spectre

But there is a spectre haunting Europe and the rest
of the industrial democratic world. It is the spectre
of 'birth death'. The key fact of our era is that the
important, free, powerful nations of the world are not
producing 2.2 children per woman – not even coming
close. In the United States the present rate is 1.8
children per woman; England is the same; France is
1.9; Japan 1.7; Italy 1.6; West Germany 1.4; Canada
1.7 going down to 1.5.

Another first

We've had all kinds of 'firsts' in this century: first
man in space; first man on the moon; first heart trans-
plant, etc. Well, here is another first: this is the first
time in history that a collection of nations has deliberately opted to drop below the necessary reproduction
level. The Western world is refusing to reproduce
itself. Consider the devastating effects if such rates
continue.

West Germany's present population is 62 million.
At its present reproduction rate, by the year 2000 it
will be 59 million; by 2050 it will be down to 38
million and by 2100 there will be only 20 million
West Germans left. Other nations will dwindle in proportion. Apart from gigantic immigration from the
Third World, this is inevitable.

You might say, "So what?" The answer is, "So
plenty!" If present populations continue to decrease,
as they must if there is not a dramatic reversal in the
birth rate, there will be a mammoth and harmful so-
cial-welfare effect. A nation with very few children
ultimately finds it impossible to pay its pension bills
to the elderly. That means sharply higher taxes (or

sharply lower benefits) resulting in social and political turbulence of a high order.

Is immigration the answer?

Immigration from other, more populous, nations might appear to be the solution. But is it? I don't think I am being racist when I say that I don't believe the West Germans, or any other nation for that matter, would welcome their country being 'taken over' by another nation – be they Polish, African, Chinese, etc. For instance, because of her diminishing birth rate, France has encouraged immigration from her former colonies in North Africa to keep up the work force. But most of the immigrants are Mohammedan from North Africa. Professor Tremblay, a French university professor, mathematically estimates that by the year 2035, France will be virtually a Moslem country. At present there are more Moslem children in French schools than Christian. The Moslems don't believe in contraception; the French do!

The final solution

What is the solution to the dwindling population? Of course the obvious one would be to return to a 'child-wanting' society and, consequently, a turning away from contraception and abortion. But I'm afraid that is not going to happen in the foreseeable future. I have a very uneasy feeling – this time in the pit of my stomach – that the solution will be sought in the murder of innocent human beings.

We began by refusing to have children. Then, when the 'unwanted' children insisted on coming along, we killed them by abortion. Between abortion and contraception the cupboard has been rendered almost bare – not enough young people to provide for the older

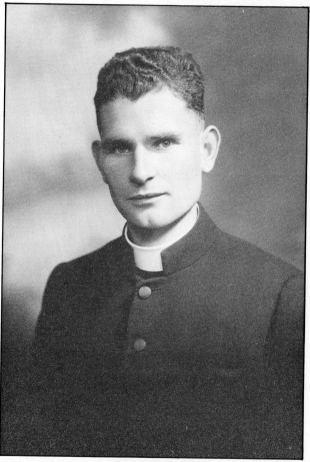

Ordination 1940

Enroute to Africa 1941

Student 1936

At Prayer 1950

With Father Peyton 1947

Kenya 1948

On Safari

Catechism Class

Home Visitation

The Mission 1969

Catechists – The Gospel on Wheels

Close Advisors

With Fr. Barney Kelly, Provincial Superior 1975

With VICS Volunteer Theresa Douros and Supporters

A Talk on the Missions to Toronto Schoolchildren 1978

You meet the nicest people 1979

Fr. Ted Colleton C.S.Sp.

folks. This result is inevitable – more inevitable than nuclear war. "The mills of God grind slowly, but they grind exceeding fine."

Euthanasia

Yes, euthanasia, man – and woman – can be very logical when it suits. If we have succeeded in rationalizing the killing of unborn babies by abortion and born babies by infanticide, why stop at granny? In a materialistic society she doesn't count. She is just one of those 'useless eaters'. And it is expensive to maintain her – so comes the inevitable query, "Why not?" That was the first question ever asked. And it was asked – and answered – in the Garden of Eden!

Population is not the problem

In the year 1798, Thomas Robert Malthus startled England and eventually the world – it took a little longer in those days – with his theory of population. In a nutshell, his theory was that the growth of population always tends to outrun the growth of production. Poverty and hunger are therefore man's inescapable fate.

Although the 'Malthusian Theory' has been proven incorrect over and over again, it still broods like a grim ghost over the shoulder of society and can be called out of retirement anytime somebody wants to start a population scare. "Unless we stop having so many kids we shall all starve and there won't be enough room on earth for all of us. By the turn of the century there will be 6 billion people in the world and where are we going to get the food to feed them all?" If this were true it would certainly be terrifying – but it is not true.

United Nations reports

Has the Creator given us natural resources to feed this vast world population or has He not? The best place to find the answer to that question is in the constant reports from the various departments of the United Nations. They have the men and the money and the tools to do the job.

Population is not the problem

Having read through some of these reports, one is led to the ineluctable conclusion that population increase is not the problem. The problem lies in the areas of production and distribution. According to the UN Food and Agriculture Organization in Rome, the world grows twice as much food every year, in grain alone, as is necessary to feed every man, woman and child in the world at present. And up to four times as much food could be produced using presently available land and technology.

How to explain hunger?

Hunger cannot be simply explained by saying, "Too many people for too little land". It can be far better explained by looking at how the available land and technology are being used and for whose benefit. An article entitled, 'Inside Oxfam' has this to say on the subject, "It is deception to make people believe that it is possible to solve problems of underdevelopment through birth control systems. The source of underdevelopment must be located in a world system which operates for the *loss of the many* and the *profit of the few.*"

Population – three examples

There must be hundreds of examples of how this unjust system works, but I shall confine myself to three. In Central America and the Caribbean more than half the agricultural land is being used to grow fruit and other crops for *export* to developed countries. In the Sahel, West Africa, even during the great drought of 1974, the production of export crops like peanuts increased considerably, according to World Bank figures, while tens of thousands of people starved. In Colombia where malnutrition is common, fertile land is used to grow $418 million worth of cut flowers a year for *export* to industrialized countries.

The fact of the matter is that only the poor starve – poverty, not lack of food, is the root of the problem. In short, economic demand is put before human demand. Another way of putting it is this: The problem is more a question of the consumption explosion in the industrialized world than of the population in the developing world.

The 'haves' versus the 'have nots'

Both actually and potentially there is plenty of food and everything else in the world to supply the present population and any foreseen increase in the future. The population of the world is divided into two kinds – the 'Haves' and the 'Have Nots'. The 'Haves' don't want to part with what they have and the 'Have Nots' have neither the voice nor the power to get what they need.

Is there any solution to the problem? Yes, but, like the food in the ground, we have to dig for it. Take your copy of the Gospel and consult St. Matthew, Chapter 25, Verses 31 to 46. The solution is 2000 years old and needs a little dusting off. But it can still work if only it is tried.

More unlearned lessons

In a recent column, I wrote about the 'unlearned lessons of history'. But there are many other unlearned lessons which have not been absorbed by society. One of them is the shocking damage which modern contraceptives have done – and are doing – to women, particularly young women.

At the 1985 National Life Conference in England, one of the speakers, a distinguished gynecologist, said this, "The 'sexual revolution' of the 60s and 70s, of which widely-available abortion is commonly regarded as an essential ingredient, is having grave effects on women's bodies – especially the bodies of young women."

He then quotes some frightening medical facts, giving very precise references for his statements. Here are a few of them.

Cancer of the cervix. *Hansard* 1984 is quoted as follows, "The treatment of women who have cancer has soared from 15 per cent in 1972 to 27 per cent in 1982. The incidence of the disease seems to be highest in patients who have been on the Pill for a considerable time."

According to the *Gynaecology Review* (December 1984), "Many more younger women are getting the disease and the death rate of these victims has increased 20 per cent. Young people should be informed of the high risk of the disease (and increased risk of death) involved in teenage sex."

Sexually Transmitted Disease (STD). The number of new cases of sexually transmitted diseases treated in England and Wales in 1968 was 180,000. By 1980, the figure had risen to 500,000. In his Annual Report for 1983, the Chief Medical Director at the Department of Health and Social Services revealed that the number of new STD cases reported by English clinics alone topped the half-million mark for the first time in history.

Pelvic Inflammatory Disease (PID). According to the British medical magazine, *Westrom Lancet*, PID, which results from sexually transmitted disease, has shown a similar increase – especially among unmarried, childless women under twenty. The risk of PID increases nearly three times among women who use an intrauterine device, especially if they have never been pregnant. PID is a major cause of infertility resulting from blocked tubes.

American research shows that, even after antibiotic treatment, infertility resulting from PID occurred in 19 per cent of cases after one infection, 31 per cent after two, and 60 per cent after three. (*American Journal of Obstetrics and Gynecology,* 1980).

Ectopic Pregnancy. According to *Contemporary Obstetrics and Gynecology* (September 1984), the incidence of ectopic pregnancies, which threaten the ability to have children later and even life itself, has more than doubled among teenagers in only five years. Increased sexual activity has greatly aggravated the problem. Intrauterine devices also increase the risk of ectopic pregnancy.

In 1973, Dr. Malcolm Potts of the International Planned Parenthood Federation – the largest pro-abortion organization in the world – predicted that abortion rates would not be reduced by an increased supply of contraceptives. On the contrary, he said, they would rise. And he was right.

Here is a quote from Dr. Judith Bury, of the pro-abortion Brook Advisory Centre in Britain, "There is overwhelming evidence that, contrary to what one might expect, the availability of contraception leads to an increase in the abortion rate."

These statements have been proved in every country in which contraception has been accepted by society. And yet the 'feminists' keep screaming for more and more contraceptives. More contraceptives mean more abortions, more sexual permissiveness, more diseases, more infertility and more ruined lives.

Young women, rise up. You have nothing to lose but your slavery to the lusts of men!

Contraception

When I return from an eight-hour flight (from Paris and Rome this time) I do not usually laugh until my metabolism has readjusted itself with the aid of eight hours rest. But I nearly did (laugh) on Sunday (December 2nd). I had plugged in the kettle just to welcome myself back when my eye fell on a photo of the Cardinal in the Sunday *Star*. The accompanying story said that a Unitarian minister, Rev. Raible stated in a sermon that he agreed with the Cardinal in his teaching on abortion but challenged his Eminence to change his teaching on the matter of contraception! That's enough to make anybody laugh. Even a cardinal cannot change the traditional teaching of his Church – taught by pope after pope for over eight hundred years – and even a Unitarian minister should know that! But the 'amusing' part is that the minister believes that if there was more contraception there would be less abortion.

No doubt the Cardinal's teaching on the wrongness of contraception – like the Pope's and my own! – is based on moral principles. But what is morally wrong is always practically damaging to humanity so I prefer to take a quick look at what I may term the 'obvious and practical damage' which this vice has done to society and particularly to women.

1978 report on contraceptives

In 1978 the Ministry of Health and Welfare in Canada

produced a report on oral contraceptives which lists eleven 'serious adverse reactions' which can befall the user of oral contraceptives. They include high blood pressure, blood clots to the eyes, lungs, abdominal organs and brain, non-fatal and fatal blood clots to the heart, liver tumors, gall bladder diseases and fetal malformations (twice the usual population risk) following the use of the pill. The report says that the pill has aged women by damaging their systems and that coronary artery disease in young women is a recent phenomenon. Among the 'less serious' results of the use of the pill, the report lists the following: mental depression, changes in libido, loss of scalp hair, impaired kidney function, etc.

At the annual meeting of the Royal College of Physicians and Surgeons of Canada, Dr. Jacques Genest, director of the Clinical Research Institute of Montreal said in his paper, "It must not be forgotten that the most widely used contraceptives, such as the Pill and intrauterine devices, act mostly by producing abortion at a very early stage and not by preventing conception as was first thought." And Rev. Raible wants these contraceptives to be used to prevent abortions!!

The Danish experiment

What has happened in Denmark over the past quarter of a century could be told of every other country which has succumbed to the myth that universal contraception will lead to an earthly paradise. If man 'lived on bread alone', Denmark would be the ideal country in which to dwell. It is the wealthiest nation on the continent of Europe; it has almost no poverty; it has cradle to grave care for all its citizens and its per capita income is probably one of the highest in Europe. Pornography was legalized in 1967. Sex education was made compulsory in schools in 1970. The children are taught all about the use of contraceptives and where to obtain them free of charge. Abortion on demand was legalized in 1973. Apart from the abortion on demand bit, Denmark would appear to be Rev. Raible's ideal of how a modern country should be administered from a sexual point of view. But let's take a glance at the results. According to official reports, forcible rape was increased 300%, venereal disease in those under twenty years of age has increased 250%, illegitimate pregnancy has doubled, the divorce rate has doubled and abortions have increased 500%. Only two things have declined during the past twenty years or so. The first is their birth rate which is at an all-time low; the other is the age of the first intercourse – with a frightening increase in cervical cancer among young girls.

Cervical cancer

Some years ago the professor of Preventive Medicine at the University of Illinois made an intensive study of the causes of cervical cancer – cancer of the uterus. Here is a summary of his findings. There were two key factors that distinguished the cancer victims from the non-cancer victims. Those with cancer of the cervix had 1) engaged in early sexual and 2) engaged in sex with many partners. He found that beginning to have sexual relations under the age of seventeen triples the risk of cancer of the womb and beginning sexual relations between the ages of seventeen and twenty doubles the risk. The research found that in order to minimize the risk of cancer of the uterus, women should start having sex later and stay with one man – did we ever hear that before!

The cancer risk of early promiscuity, according to

Dr. Eugene Diamond, professor of Pediatrics at Loyola University, is universally accepted in medical circles. It is virtually incontrovertible. And if there is one thing that has encouraged and increased teenage promiscuity it is surely the easy access to contraceptives. Dr. Robert Kissinger of Harvard Medical School, predicts that adolescent promiscuity will lead to a whole new generation of infertile women. Reporting to the American College of Surgeons Clinical Congress a few years ago, this same doctor made a very humble and courageous statement. He said, "About ten years ago I declared that the pill would not lead to promiscuity. Well, I was wrong. Anyone who treats patients for infertility must be alarmed at the marked increase over the last five years of virulent gonorrhea with infection of the tubes, tubal adhesions and probably permanent infertility."

When Pope Paul VI published his famous encyclical, *Humanae Vitae,* he probably became a member of the 'top ten' most unpopular people in the world. Not only did the non-Catholic world castigate him, but many of his own priests, theologians and lay people cast stones. One of the priests who opposed the Pope was Father Arthur McNally. In 1976, as editor of the *Sign Magazine*, Fr. McNally wrote as follows, "An army of theologians, psychologists and sociologists raised a great cry. Pastors and priests (myself included) read their impassioned criticisms and, convinced by their professional credentials, many of us concluded that the Pope must be wrong. When I look back over what I have written about birth control and how I have handled it in the confessional and in counselling, I'm not very proud of my record." He is just one of many who have realized how wrong they were, but do not have either the humility or the courage to admit their error.

I would like to conclude by 'humbly' suggesting that it is not Cardinal Carter but Rev. Raible who needs to change his views on contraception!

The return of Mr. Turner

Politics as politics have never interested me. I have lived as a citizen in three countries and have never belonged to a political party in any one of them. But I do come to life when moral and political issues blend into one, and this has certainly occurred in Canada with regard to abortion. So, I must admit that I am vitally interested in who will be the next prime minister of Canada, and in what position he or she will take on the rights of the unborn.

Although I was not in Canada in 1969 when the law was passed which left the unborn child virtually unprotected, I have read a great deal about how it came into being. Next to Mr. Pierre Trudeau who framed the bill, it was Mr. John Turner, as Minister of Justice, who was principally responsible for presenting it to Parliament.

Taxpayers and abortion

I have read that Mr. Turner considered he was 'merely' legalizing what was already a 'medical' practice – the killing of a few unborn babies each year by abortion. According to *Hansard*, Mr. Turner was asked in the House if taxpayers' money would pay for abortions, and he replied, "Oh, no!"

Since that time – as a direct result of Mr. Turner's infamous bill – the 'few thousand' babies aborted annually have swollen to more than 60,000, and the

Canadian taxpayer (no matter how opposed to abortion he or she may be) foots the bill for this unspeakable crime.

Surely, in the nine years he has been away from politics, Mr. Turner would have realized the appalling results of his Bill C-150. He must have read or heard that the hospital committees set up as a result of his Bill are a disaster for the unborn child. According to the Badgley Report, tabled in the House of Commons on February 9, 1977, many physicians in Canada "openly acknowledged that their diagnoses for mental health were given for purposes of expediency and they could not be considered as a valid assessment of an abortion patient's state of mental health." (page 212).

Mr. Turner is a 'practising Catholic' (please don't ask me to define *that*) and he cannot be ignorant of the strong position taken by his Pope and by the Second Vatican Council. I quote, "Abortion is an abominable crime... to attack unborn life at any moment from its conception is to undermine the whole moral order which is the true guardian of the well-being of man."

As one who attends Mass every Sunday and – so I am told – is a lector in his church, Mr. Turner cannot be unaware of the statements of the Catholic Bishops of Ontario. Here is just one: "Every human being is unique and priceless because made by God in the image and likeness of God. Every human life – let there be no mistake – is therefore fit to live for as long as the Lord of all life may choose. In the world designed by God there can be no such thing as a human being unwanted, unloved or useless." Does Mr. Turner believe this?

100

Casual about death

On the day Mr. Turner officially entered the race for leader of the Liberal Party, I watched his interview with Barbara Frum of CBC's 'The Journal'. He was asked, "Would you, as Prime Minister, attempt to limit the abortion law?" I held my breath – but not for very long. Mr. Turner didn't bat an eyelid. This is, in substance, what he answered, "I was the one who put the bill through in 1969. I think there must be cases when abortion is justified – in the case of the life or health of the mother. I think that therapeutic abortion is a fair compromise." That was all…

The reply was as casual as if he had been asked, "Would you change the speed limit on Highway 401?" The impression one got was that over 60,000 Canadian babies done to death each year – more than one million since Mr. Turner's Bill changed the law – were not worth discussing. Unemployment is, of course, the priority with Mr. Turner, and it certainly should be a priority. But the unemployed have votes, the unborn do not. Could that fact be significant?

Before somebody comes up with the objection, "But you are mixing religion with politics", I would like to submit a prior question: "How many Gods can one man serve?"

Editors' note: – This column was written upon the return to federal politics of John Turner, Prime Minister of Canada in 1984.

A 'multiple' issue

The passing of Bill C-169 on October 25, 1983, appears to be a concerted attempt, on the part of the three federal parties, to muzzle free speech during future elections. The substance of the Bill has been examined and explained in previous issues of *The Interim*, so I presume that readers are aware of its contents.

It is couched in the usual legalistic terms, which only legal people understand fully, but, with a little help, most of us can grasp its more obvious implications. From my reading, I gather that Canadian citizens are so effectively gagged that it would be impossible to challenge any candidate during the 60 days of the election period without risking a fine of up to $5,000 or a 5-year jail term.

What can we do?

The National Citizens' Coalition has commenced legal proceedings, arguing that the Bill contravenes the Charter of Rights. We hope and pray that they may succeed in restoring some of our freedom of speech and action which has been so outrageously denied by this Bill. But, suppose they do not succeed. Is there anything we can do to have our principles at least heard? I think there is.

The law does not take effect until an election has been declared and an election has not yet been declared. So there is some time at your disposal to challenge your candidates on any issue you please, particularly on how they stand on the biggest issue of all – the protection of the unborn.

I strongly suggest that all who profess to be pro-life take the time either to phone or write to their candidates, asking them where they stand – or sit – on this paramount question. If they reply saying how much they appreciated your letter or call but give 'both sides' of the question and explain that the matter is so complex that it is impossible to solve it in the present 'political climate', don't let them get away with such meaningless and insulting jargon.

No 'ifs' and 'buts'

I have had such letters from the Prime Minister on down, and they all add up to one big 'zero'. The only effective reaction is to write back saying that the issue of abortion is just about as complicated as the issues of murder, rape, or bank robbery!

In reply to the question, "What is your stand on the issue of rape?" would the candidate be prepared to stand before an assembly of women and say, "Well, I think it is a very complex question, and in certain circumstances I think that rape should be both legal and justified." On the question of killing an innocent human being there are no 'ifs' or 'buts'. Your candidate is either for or against abortion and make him or her say which.

If any candidates refuse to give a definite answer, tell them that 'fence-sitters' on the most vital issue of the century – in the words of the Gospel – deserve to be vomited out of the mouth.

You will probably get the usual 'single-issue politics' bilge. Well, over one million dead Canadians in fifteen years is a very 'multiple' issue.

Editor' note: – Bill C-169 was ruled unlawful by the Supreme Court of Alberta.

Gentlemen, the President of the United States

Almost every evening we watch pictures of President Reagan on the TV and hear discussions for or against his political policies and actions. I have to confess to being a 'political dummy' who knows very little about economic or social problems. I take an interest in politics only when there is a moral issue at stake. Whether the President is right in his policies regarding Soviet Russia or the Middle East or Central America I do not know. But one thing I do know is this. President Reagan is correct in his position on the Right to Life issue.

The conscience of the nation

In a powerful article entitled, "Abortion and the Conscience of the Nation" published in the June 1983 issue of the *Human Life Review*, (reprinted with permission in the *INTERIM* June '83 -ed.), the President pulls no punches and makes no apologies for his stand. Apart from Pope John Paul II, no world leader has come out with such strong and unyielding statements against abortion as the current president of the United States.

Canada take heed

In view of the tragic happenings in Canada over the past fourteen years and particularly over the past few months, we have much to learn from the 'American scene'. So, I shall quote some salient statements from the article in question. These are President Reagan's own words: "But the consequences of this decision (Supreme Court 1973) are obvious. Since 1973 more than 15 million unborn children have had their lives snuffed out by legalized abortions. That is over ten times the number of Americans lost in all our nation's wars."

The value of human life

"We cannot diminish the value of one category of human life – the unborn – without diminishing the value of all human life. We saw tragic proof of this truism last year when the Indiana courts allowed the starvation of 'Baby Doe' – because the child had Down's Syndrome."

The benefit of the doubt

"I have often said that when we talk about abortion we are talking about two lives – the life of the mother and the life of the unborn child – I have also said that anyone who doesn't feel sure whether we are talking about a second human life should clearly give **life** the benefit of the doubt. If you don't know whether a body is alive or dead, you would never bury it."

The crime of being retarded

The President continues, "A doctor testified to the presiding judge that, even with his physical problem corrected, Baby Doe would have a 'non-existent' possibility for a 'minimally adequate quality of life'. The judge let Baby Doe starve to death and the Indiana Court sanctioned his decision. In other words, retardation is a crime deserving the penalty of death."

Handicapped newborns protected by law

"I have directed the Departments of Justice and HHS to apply civil rights regulations to protect handicapped newborns. All hospitals receiving federal funds must post notices which clearly state that failure to feed handicapped babies is prohibited by federal law. The basic issue is whether to value and protect the lives of the handicapped; whether to recognize the sanctity of human life. This is the basic issue that underlies the question of abortion."

Senate hearings 1981

"The Senate Hearings on the beginning of human life brought out the basic issue more clearly than ever before. The many medical and scientific witnesses who testified, disagreed on many things, but not on the scientific evidence that the unborn child is alive, is a distinct individual and is a member of the human species."

The need for prayer

The President concludes, "I have often said we need to join in prayer to bring protection to the unborn. Prayer and action are needed to uphold the sanctity of human life. I believe it will not be possible to accomplish our work, the work of saving lives, without being a soul at prayer."

THANK YOU MR. PRESIDENT.

...and promises to keep

I like Ontario Premier Mr. David Peterson. I haven't met him personally but, seeing him on television, I think he is a man to whom I could relate. He has a sensitive, intelligent face, a gracious manner and there is no trace of arrogance in his bearing. He also gives the impression of being a 'family man', with an attractive wife and beautiful children.

Having said all that — and said it sincerely — I have to add that I am sadly disappointed in Mr. Peterson's performance to date on what *Newsweek* has described as "the burning issue of the eighties." Needless to say, the issue is abortion.

Before the election

Before the Ontario provincial election (May 1985), Campaign Life wrote to Mr. Peterson, asking him if he and his party were against the establishment of freestanding abortion clinics — such as the one on Harbord Street. Here is an exact copy of Mr. Peterson's reply:

> "I am pleased to take the opportunity to outline my party's position on the issue of freestanding abortion clinics. In response to your questionnaire, "Yes, the Ontario Liberal Party is opposed to the establishment of freestanding abortion clinics throughout Ontario.
>
> "Yes, if elected I will support a government's

108

measures to close the existing abortion clinic in Toronto."
(Signed) "Sincerely, David Peterson."

On the strength of that unequivocal assurance, Mr. Peterson and his party were supported by many people who are devoted to the cause of saving the lives of unborn babies.

After the election

But Mr. Peterson has not kept his promises. There is no sign of the Harbord Street abortuary being closed and the excuse (given several times by Mr. Peterson) is that nothing can be done while the case is before the courts.

This is not true. I am not a lawyer, but I have consulted lawyers and am assured that the government has the power to close the clinic. So, the kindest thing I can say about Mr. Peterson is that he doesn't know the law – and he should.

The killing still goes on

During all this time, the killing still goes on! Human beings are being killed daily at the Harbord Street "clinic" and Mr. Peterson knows it. It is boring to open the newspapers daily and read more and more accusations made by the Federal opposition parties to the effect that the Prime Minister is not keeping his election promises and that his ministers are not telling the truth on vital issues. Now we have this very personable provincial premier sloughing off questions by Pro-Life people with legal verbiage – signifying nothing!

Must politics inevitably corrode?

Apart from John Sweeney, is there such a creature as an honest, truthful, promise-keeping politician in Ontario? If there is, would he/she please stand up and be counted?

A government's first duty is the protection of its people, irrespective of how rich or poor, well or ill, large or small, they may be. The exploitation of the poor in the interests of the rich, is not nearly as unjust as the killing of the unborn in the imagined interest of the born.

I am just as opposed to the abortions that are being performed in hospitals as I am to those being performed in the Harbord Street "clinic." But Mr. Peterson would be up against the federal law if he tried to stop the hospital abortions. However, here in his own province and, one might add, almost on his own doorstep, an illegal abortion mill is thriving. According to its principal owner and manager, more than 1,600 babies have been killed since it reopened less than a year ago. Not only does the government refuse to close it, but the Attorney General – who supports the concept of abortion on demand – protects it with the police force.

A model of statesmanship

Sorry, Mr. Peterson. Immediately after the election, I would have been proud to point you out anywhere in the world as the premier of my province. But not today. You have promises to keep and you have not kept them. There are lives you could have saved and you haven't saved them.

Remember the last words of Sir Thomas More as he stood on the scaffold, "I die the King's good servant, but God's first." If he had taken the position which you have, neither you nor I would be aware that he lived – or died!

A Daniel
come to judgment

When I first became a member of the Right to Life
Speakers' Bureau, I was warned that I should not use
the term 'murder' when referring to an abortion. It
was too 'judgmental', I was told. I did not agree but,
being the subservient creature that I am, I obeyed.

I euphemistically spoke of the 'the killing of the
unborn'. I admit that the word murder did sometimes
escape from my lips when speaking in the pulpit –
when I threw discretion to the winds and decided I
had to do something to wake up the congregation.

Courage from the bench

But now – for the first time in Canadian history – a
judge has had the courage to call abortion exactly
what it is – murder. *Editor's Note: Ontario Provincial
Court Judge Arthur Meen heard a case in 1985 in
which fourteen pro-life demonstrators were charged
with trespassing when they held sit-ins on the front
steps of Morgentaler's Toronto abortuary. In the course
of his decision Judge Meen stated "The fact remains
that human lives were being aborted on the dates in
question, that the defendants knew this was occurring
and that they were endeavouring to put a stop to it.
That is to say, they were doing whatever they could
to stop the loss of human life. And it was not as
though those human lives were being taken lawfully,
for, in fact, the Clinic was operating outside the law,
and such was therefore murder."*

We have become accustomed to speakers of almost every ilk – doctors, lawyers, social workers, pro-abortionists, politicians – engaging in semantic calisthenics in order to avoid being trapped in legal jargon.

They call abortion 'the expulsion of the fetus', or 'the emptying of the uterus'. The child is referred to as 'an unwanted pregnancy'. In other words, call it anything but what it is – the murder of a human being. It is something like calling a spade 'an instrument for digging', or defining rape as 'the releasing of sexual tensions through the instrumentality of an unwilling female person'. Call a spade anything you wish, but it still remains a spade. Call rape by any other name and it is still rape. Euphemize murder by the use of any semantic gymnastics you can conjure up, but it is still murder.

Deliberate killing

But is abortion murder? Of course it is! If murder is the deliberate killing of an innocent human being, then abortion is murder and the abortionist is a murderer. How he or she stands subjectively in the sight of Almighty God is not for me to judge. But objectively speaking, and that's the way I'm speaking, an abortionist deliberately takes the life of an innocent human being and, in so doing, he commits first-degree murder.

The attorney general

I think what prompted me to write this particular column (on the morning of the 25th of September) was a radio announcement, quoting the Ontario Attorney General, Mr. Ian Scott. He was reported to have said words to the effect that Judge Meen will not be criticised officially for his statement that abortion is

113

murder. The Supreme Court will decide that question. The case involved fourteen demonstrators who sat on abortuary steps to prevent abortions in December 1984. The Pro-Lifers were charged with trespassing.

So, abortion could be murder in one country and a simple operation in another. God's commandment, "Thou shalt not kill", is obsolete and the Supreme Court judges take the place of the Creator.

If I were to commit a murder, it is possible that a clever lawyer could succeed in having the court declare me innocent by some technical point of law. But I would still be a murderer with the blood of a human being on my hands. And, like Lady Macbeth, "All the perfumes of Arabia" – and certainly not all the courts of Canada – could not remove the stain of blood from my hands.

Judge Meen

And so, Judge Meen, although I never heard of you until the other day and although I know nothing of your views on other matters, I salute you as a just and honourable judge and a man with the courage of his convictions. We need more like you.

'One issue' people?

One of the most common stones thrown at 'pro-lifers' is that we are 'One Issue' people. We don't care about any other issue except abortion; we are not interested in what happens to babies who are born into difficult circumstances; and we do nothing for pregnant mothers either before their babies are born or afterwards.

Sign on the dotted line

To give an example: one day somebody approached the picketers outside the Morgentaler abortuary and challenged them to sign a document. It stated that they were pledging themselves to support a baby from birth to maturity. They were to sign on the dotted line as a token of their concern for more than the baby in the womb.

Naturally, nobody was dumb enough to sign this document and Lois Sweet used this fact in an extremely distasteful article which she wrote in the *Toronto Star*, to prove that 'Pro-Lifers' are not interested in anyone but the baby in the womb.

How do we answer this charge?

I suppose one reply would be to simply say that the accusation is false. But my experience is that parallel examples are always useful. Let us turn to the large field of modern medicine.

There are all kinds of specialists these days and they seem to be increasing. There are heart specialists and cancer specialists and eye specialists and ear specialists, etc. But we don't accuse the heart specialist of not being interested in the brain, or the eye specialist of not being concerned about the ears. Each one does his own thing and if they all do their part the entire human body will be catered for. But if they all specialize in the eyes, who will look after the ears? And if they all concentrate on ears, who will restore our sight? A scientist who is involved in research on leukemia is not chided for ignoring other deadly diseases. People know that there are other specialists who deal with the varied problems to which the flesh is heir.

Interests must be diversified

Applying the same principle to everyday living, suppose all men were mailmen. Who would deal with crime or impaired driving? If all store keepers were grocers, where would we get our clothes? People don't abuse the grocer and accuse him of not being interested in the naked nor do they abuse the tailor for neglecting the hungry. I haven't heard of the nuclear freeze supporters being accused of not being concerned about the handicapped. Yet, they are all 'one issue' people in the context of what they do for society.

Perhaps the best way to sum it all up is this. If everybody did everything, society would be in an even worse mess than it is! We all need each other's talents, but, for society to achieve any kind of efficiency, these talents must be allowed to bloom in the soil which suits them.

There are limits
to what people can do

Certainly it is imperative for all of us to be aware that injustice takes many different forms, has many ugly heads and that there is much work to be done. But no one can be actively involved in solving every problem. Each one of us has limited resources of time, energy and money.

I know many people who are actively engaged in such necessary works as helping the handicapped, supporting pregnant women, feeding the hungry, etc. There are people who volunteer to go to foreign countries to help in health, education and agriculture.

I feel called to help as a volunteer in the Pro-Life Movement. To me, the most important aspect of social work is the defence of the unborn, but I would be very unjust and uncharitable if I were to assume that people who feel called to dedicate themselves to other forms of charity were not interested in the baby in the womb. Of course they are interested, but their talents lie in different fields of endeavour.

St. Paul

Perhaps St. Paul puts what I have said more succinctly when he says, "If the whole body were the eye, where would be the hearing? And if the whole body were the hearing, where would be the smelling? But God has so adjusted the body – that there may be no discord but that the members may have the same care for each other. If one member suffers, all suffer together; if one member is honoured, all rejoice together."

Thank you, Paul. I couldn't have put it better myself!

How should I vote?

It is very difficult to imagine what one isn't! But I am going to try just for a few moments.

Act 1 – The Atheist

I am an atheist and in the coming election I want to vote for what is best for Canada. I'm not emotionally attached to any of the three parties so, in practice, I am reduced to looking at the candidates who are standing in my riding.

Enter the pro-lifers

Some pro-life group has brought the abortion issue to my notice. I never really thought much about it before but according to this leaflet over one million Canadian babies have been killed by abortion in a dozen years. Good God! (sorry I forgot, there is no god).

Sheer Economics

From the point of view of sheer economics this cannot be good for any country. One million less people in a country means one million less breakfasts, lunches and dinners every day – with loss of employment for all the people who produce them. It must mean thousands of teachers out of employment, ten million less pairs of shoes, socks, shirts, dresses, pants etc., over the years. It probably means half a million less cars purchased and serviced not to speak of bicycles, books and ice creams.

118

A vanishing population

The leaflet also reminds me that in order to barely replace its population a nation must have at the very least a reproduction rate of 2.2 children per married couple. In Canada the present reproduction rate is something like 1.4 children per couple. This means that as the old people get older there will not be enough young people in the work force to support them. Somehow it doesn't appear to be a very sound economic system! I shall have to find out the positions of the candidates in my riding before I cast my vote and I certainly shall not vote for a pro-abortionist. (Curtain).

Act 2 – The Christian

I'm a Christian but not a Catholic. I firmly believe in God and also in Jesus Christ. But my Church has been wishy-washy on the abortion issue. The leaders have not taken a firm stand and given leadership to their flocks. Only the Roman Catholics and the Pentecostal Assemblies have spoken out and told the people what abortion really means – the killing of a human being.

To thy own self be true

If this is correct – and science seems to have proved it beyond a doubt – how can I claim to be a follower of Christ and support a candidate who is going to vote in Parliament for abortion on demand? I know I can attend my Church and look like a 'good Christian' (I wonder what that means?) but if I have neither the courage nor the Christian principles to oppose those who want more than one million babies killed during the next twelve years, can I call myself a Christian? I know the answer to that question! (Curtain).

Act 3 – The Roman Catholic

I'm a Catholic – not as good as I should be perhaps. I attend Mass, and receive Holy Communion and abide by the teachings of the Church. Should my religion influence the way I vote? From a mere political point of view it should not, but suppose there is a moral issue – what then? Abortion certainly is a moral issue! Since the second century the Church has always condemned abortion as the killing of a potential or an actual human being. Of course in those days they knew nothing about genetics. But now science teaches us that the 'fetus' is a human being from the moment of conception. So, abortion at any stage must mean the killing of a human being.

Recent statements of the Church

In recent times the Vatican Council, the Popes, the Bishops and the New Code of Canon Law have condemned abortion in terms which are crystal clear. The present Pope has said that Catholic lawmakers must take a stand against laws which favour abortion.

Who has changed?

The pro-abortionists – 'pro-choice' is a euphemistic term for 'pro-abortion' – say that this is a 'Catholic issue'. But up to about forty years ago the laws of every country forbade abortion. It is only within the past fifteen years that Canada has made it legal to kill the unborn. So, who has changed? The Church or society? This is a rhetorical question.

The future

In twenty years from now society will make it legal to perhaps smother grandparents who have become expensive and inconvenient or to poison disobedient

120

and 'unwanted' children or to pierce the hearts of
alcoholic husbands (or wives) or, in general, to get
rid of anybody who does not measure up to a certain
'quality of life' decided by a committee set up by the
state. It all sounds ridiculous but it isn't! We are doing
all these things to the 'unborn' – and they would not
have been tolerated forty years ago. So how do we
know we won't be doing the same to the 'born' thirty
years from now?

How shall I vote as a Catholic?

I have come to a decision. I cannot vote for a pro
abortion candidate. If I did so I would have to stop
going to Mass and leave the Church – or stop facing
myself in the mirror every morning!

Final Curtain.

Are we doing enough?

At an informal meeting the other day a number of pro-life people were discussing what we could do to stop the daily killing of unborn babies at the Morgentaler abortuary. The picketing was assessed and some felt that it is not effective enough when weighed against the amount of input by so few dedicated people. It is estimated that more than one hundred babies have been done to death since the 'clinic' opened – while the police stand guard to protect the criminals inside from possible interference on the part of the 'fanatics' outside. These 'fanatics' are the people who are 'misguided' enough to believe that a defenceless baby has a right not to be killed by anyone – and certainly not with the silent consent of the government and the people of Ontario.

The politicians

Some thought that more pressure should be brought to bear on the politicians who had signed – before the election – that they would support government measures to have the existing 'clinic' closed. Now they have been elected but the government's reply when approached is, "The matter is before the courts and nothing can be done until a decision is reached."

If Canada were invaded

I wonder if this would be their answer if Canada were invaded by a foreign power and an international court

122

had been set up to decide on the justice or otherwise of the invasion. Would the government, the army and the police sit around discussing the legality of the situation while the enemy wrought havoc among the people? Some readers must be old enough to remember the Second World War. If they were in Britain at the time – as I happened to be – they will recall that the entire Parliament, all political parties and the population were solidly behind the Prime Minister in attempting to prevent the enemy from invading the country.

We are at war

The only difference, in principle, between that War and the present situation in Canada is this. In the Second World war the enemy was from outside. In the present Canadian Civil War the enemy is here inside Canada and the victims are the unborn Canadians who cannot defend themselves.

Is this an outlandish comparison?

If this comparison sounds 'outlandish', 'fanatical' and/or 'stupid', let's take a look at some statistics. In the six years of World War II, 39,000 Canadians were killed by the enemy. Mathematically speaking, this would mean that, at the same rate, 65,000 Canadians would have been killed in ten years. But in the ten years between 1969 and 1979, more than one million Canadian babies were killed by abortion. This is a civil war between the born and the unborn of Canada. Has that thought ever occurred to you?

Out of sight, out of mind

I think one reason so many people who claim to be against abortion in theory, do nothing in practice, is that they are not emotionally affected by what they do not see. For instance, if we only read about the American hostages or the crash of the Indian plane, perhaps we would not be so angry about these terrorist actions. But the TV screen makes sure that we see the hostages in captivity with guns pointed at their heads, and dead bodies floating in the ocean, and relatives in tears, and we have become emotionally and personally involved in the particular tragedy.

Every picture tells a story

The old sayings, "Every picture tells a story", or "A picture is worth a thousand words", are very valid in the present situation. I believe that if every woman who is contemplating aborting her child were to see *The Silent Scream*, abortions would be considerably lessened. The sight of a baby being torn apart in its mother's womb has far more impact than simply hearing or reading about it. But the fact remains the same – a tortured, battered, abused and murdered human being.

A practical example

I have never witnessed an abortion and I hope I never shall. I would have to be bound hand and foot and gagged! But I did get close to one a few days ago. I paid a visit to the picketers at the abortuary on Harbord Street. I went around to the back of the 'clinic' where the women enter for their abortions. It was about 4 p.m. and I was chatting to some of the picketers. The door opened and a little girl who looked about 14 came out accompanied by a very well-groomed lady, who could have been her grandmother. The girl was smiling and looked happy. She reminded me of a kid who had received a cabbage patch doll

124

for Christmas. She got into a small car driven by a younger woman. Then a large limousine drew into the lane. The older lady stepped in and was whisked away, followed by the other car.

I asked the picketers if they thought the girl had had an abortion. They said, "Why, of course. She's been in there for several hours." I am not often rendered speechless, but on this occasion I was. Of course, I have known for years that abortions are performed even on fourteen-year-old girls. But somehow, the sight of this little girl spoke louder than a thousand words. A young girl, whose life can never be the same; a dead baby and – somewhere out there – a boy 'friend'.

I usually sleep rather well – but that night I didn't.

I hate picketing

Join the club, so do I! Through all the years of my conscious life, I have looked askance at picketers. Rallies are different. Whenever I saw a crowd of a few thousand people protesting something or defending something, I often felt I could join them and get lost in the throng. But ten or twenty people walking up and down with placards drove me to the other side of the street with the unspoken question, "What are those nuts protesting about anyhow?"

If I had been told ten or twelve years ago that I would be seen walking up and down holding a placard, together with a score of other people, I would have said, "Not on your life. I'm not made that way." My attitude was, "I'll talk about a cause; I'll write about a cause; I'll subscribe to a cause; I might even die for a cause. But don't ask me to walk up and down with a placard."

The abortuary

Then came the Morgentaler abortuary. In a busy street in Metro Toronto, a doctor (who, by his profession, is pledged to save lives and heal) sets up 'business' in an ordinary house. And his 'business' is the killing of innocent human beings, unborn babies.

When the picketing began – I can't even remember who organized it – I felt that, like British Justice, I should be 'seen', just to let it be known which side

126

I am on. So I went to the 'Clinic' on Harbord Street and made sure that I was 'seen'. But I did not take up a placard. I talked to the people and shook hands with them – like a politician before an election. I encouraged them and they told me that it was good to see a priest there. I tried to look modest but I did not take up a placard. After all, I'm a priest and priests are not expected to do things like that!

The picketers

The people on the picket were a very mixed group. There were old people and young people; men and women, girls and boys; a young mother with a two-month-old baby; a handicapped youth.

There were also four or five police officers guarding the 'Clinic'. I couldn't help feeling sad looking at these fine young men who are probably fathers of babies themselves. They had joined the force to 'protect the people'. And here they are protecting the people who are killing the people – and getting paid for it.

Didn't Shakespeare say, "Oh! Judgment thou hath fled to brutish beasts and men have lost their reason?" Of course, their argument would be that they are simply doing their job and obeying orders. It doesn't sound a bad argument – especially if a man has a wife and family – but I wondered what I would do if my Bishop ordered me to go to a church and preach against the Gospel.

A performing bear?

Then up came a lady with a sweet smile and she said, "Father, would you mind holding this placard? I just want to get a cup of coffee." Oh boy! That was when

127

I found myself walking round and holding a placard which said, "Babies are people too". I felt like a performing bear (choose your own animal) in a circus and hoped that none of my friends would pass by and see me. After all, I am a priest you know!

It is a busy street and traffic is relatively heavy. Some drivers blew their horns and gave us the 'thumbs up' sign, which was encouraging. But a few deliberately slowed down and used names and language which are not found in the best dictionaries and which *The Interim* would not print.

Fools for Christ

So, here I am – not as often as other people – picketing the abortuary. Walking round and round, saying the Rosary and feeling a fool. But, wait a minute. Didn't St. Paul say something about being "Fools for Christ"? Yes, he did and that's the answer.

If I were an atheist or an agnostic, I would not be here. If I didn't believe in a God Who made every human being in His own image and likeness, I wouldn't see any difference between a baby and a baboon. And even if I believed in God but didn't know or didn't believe that He died on a cross for every one of these unborn babies, I wouldn't see that they had any special value – at least not enough to make me picket in their defence.

To get back to St. Paul. I'm almost certain that it was he who also said, "Caritas Christi urget nos". That might be loosely translated thus, "The love of Christ makes us get off our butts and do something." It sure does.

It made me get off my butt and do something I never thought anything would make me do – walk around in a circle holding a placard and feeling like a picketing panda!

Padlocking

What's the point of padlocking the abortuary? I am sure that a number of my friends, who have been kind enough to express their encouragement and support are asking themselves that question. So, I thought a few of my ideas might be helpful.

Obviously locking the gate of the 'clinic' will not stop abortions. It might delay one or two. With the right instrument it doesn't take more than three minutes to cut the chain. So, what good does it do?

Symbolism

If we stop to analyse many of our daily habits we shall realize that symbolism plays a tremendous part in the living of our everyday lives. A handshake in itself is a very small action. But its true significance can be assessed by its refusal. The refusal to shake hands can and often does mean the breaking of a life-long friendship.

Just suppose, for instance, that President Reagan were to publicly refuse to clasp the outstretched hand of Mr. Mulroney. Canada would consider it a colossal insult, not only to the Prime Minister, but to Canada as a nation. A handshake symbolically says, "I am your friend." The refusal symbolically says, "I reject your friendship." As a matter of historical interest, the reason we clasp each other's right hand stems from the fact that the sword was traditionally worn at the left hip. So, giving each other the right hand meant, "Don't worry, I can't draw my sword while you are holding my right hand – we are friends."

We can apply the same principle to many of our mutual actions – a smile, a scowl, a salute, a thumbs-up sign. As physical actions, they are small and insignificant. But as symbols of our feelings towards people and nations, they not only speak volumes but can unleash the dogs of war.

A few more examples

Let's take the example of the burning of the American flag in Nicaragua. Such an action does not mean that America grinds to a halt. But the flag is the symbol of everything for which America stands. Therefore the burning of it can be, and is, the most powerful way of telling America, "We don't like you. We hate you. Keep out of our country."

The refusal of a junior officer to raise his right hand about a foot and touch the side of his head when passing a senior officer in the army could mean court martial and a few days in the 'slammer'. Why? Because the refusal to salute symbolizes a lack of respect for authority.

Back to the gate

But let's get back to the gate – the police will be waiting to greet us! What am I symbolically saying when I lock or attempt to lock the "clinic" gate? Whether or not I succeed in locking it is not important. It is the symbolism that matters.

What I am saying to the public of Toronto is this. "This house is a bastion of everything that is evil. The open gate means, 'Come in and have your baby

131

murdered.' By locking the gate, I am symbolically and publicly expressing my conviction that this house of death should be closed and its gate locked so that the lives of at least some unborn babies may be spared."

It says a lot more

But I am saying much more than that. I am challenging the Attorney General – who took an oath to uphold the law – to observe his oath of office. The "clinic" is not only immoral, it is illegal – it is a public breach of Section 251 of the Criminal Code. I am also showing my contempt for the action of the Commissioner of Police. His officers, on his orders, leap to arrest me for locking a gate; while they protect the murderers who tear babies to pieces inside the 'clinic'! I am also challenging the Premier – who claims he is anti-abortion – to take a stand in defence of the lives of the weakest members of the province. If he cannot do this – as he claims he cannot – then I think he should resign.

And even more

But I am also saying this. If my feeble efforts to make the public aware of the terrible crimes that are being committed in that house of death mean that I end up in jail, that I accept. We must live with the consequences of our decisions. I love my personal freedom too much to suggest that I would enjoy being in prison. I love my private room, my comfortable bed and my well-cooked meals too much to pretend that I would surrender them with a careless shrug.

But these creature comforts are the decorations of life – not life itself! When weighed in the balance against a public witness to the sacredness of human life and the rights of the unborn, they are but 'sounding brass and tinkling cymbal'. And here I rest my case!

What price?

It was Abraham Lincoln who gave posterity the famous saying, "You can fool all the people some of the time and some of the people all the time, but you can't fool all the people all the time." If he had said "please" instead of "fool" it would be just as true – in fact more so.

I have never tried to please all the people all the time and I don't intend to start now. But I was both interested and amused at the reactions to my locking the gate of the abortion clinic.

I have received – both verbally and in writing – such accolades as, "It is great to see our priests showing leadership" and "If everybody had your courage that 'so-and-so' clinic would have been closed long ago."

I received congratulations even from Ireland and Boston, where the incident had been reported in the Catholic papers.

But these laudatory statements were balanced by others of a derogatory kind such as, "It is nearly time you got sense," or, "It is a bad example for ministers of religion to break the law", and, "I admire your courage but you have no right to interfere with private property."

Obligation to challenge

When remarks are complimentary I try to look modest – which I find almost impossible – and attempt to change the subject, hoping that I will not succeed. But when they are otherwise I feel an obligation to challenge them.

I usually begin with a question such as, "Suppose you saw a six-year-old child being carried into a house and knew for certain – or at least suspected – that he or she was going to be murdered, what would you do? Would you decide that you couldn't do anything because it was private property? Would you decide that if the parents wanted him or her murdered, it was their business and not yours? Or would you feel that it was improper to impose your moral values on the murderers inside, who are being handsomely paid for doing the murders and, therefore, felt it was morally defensible to take the life of an innocent child?"

There's no difference

When people who claim to be Christians and particularly if they are Catholics, who have such clear teaching from their Church, try to tell me that there is a difference – in principle – between murdering a six-year-old child and murdering an unborn baby, I must admit that my patience begins to wear thin.

Since the breaking of the genetic code – in the nineteen fifties – there is no doubt in the minds of *honest* scientists – please note the adjective – that human life begins at conception. Therefore, abortion is murder just as surely as the killing of a six-year-old child or an eighty-year-old person. Euphemistic terms do not change moral facts!

135

Trespassing

I was listening to a Pro-Life tape the other day and the speaker – who has been in court also in the U.S. for entering an abortion clinic – made what I have been trying to say clearer. He asked, "Suppose you were passing a private house and you saw a man or a woman drowning their baby in the swimming pool, would you just pass by because there was a notice saying, 'Private property. No trespassing'? Suppose you were called to court as a witness and were asked by the judge, 'Why did you not try to save the child?' How would you feel if your only reply was, 'I could not bring myself to break the law against trespassing!'"

I know I should feel bitterly ashamed and a miserable coward.

If we can rush into a private house to save a baby from death by drowning, why can't we rush to save one from being murdered? I can't see a difference.

The other day somebody asked me, "But are you really prepared to go to jail?" I think I was supposed to say, "Oh well, there are limits somewhere." However, my reply seemed to shock him. I said, "If I knew that the sentence for locking that gate was public hanging, I still would have locked it – and I shall lock it again."

In good company

Far greater men than I have languished in jail for far lesser causes – Cardinal Stepinac of Yugoslavia, Cardinal Mindszenty of Hungary, Cardinal Beran of Czechoslovakia – all in my lifetime. Nobler men and women than I shall ever be, have made the supreme

136

sacrifice in defence of their convictions – starting on Calvary.

In our own day, Archbishop Romero of El Salvador was slain at the altar for just one reason – he would not be silenced by threats.

No apology

And so, I am not ashamed of the historical company in which I find myself. Nobody will convince me that there is a more important issue than the daily murder of our unborn children. The saving of those lives is in itself of paramount importance. But that is not all.

Abortion destroys the very fibre of a nation. It is the most shocking degradation of womanhood and motherhood. A society that condones abortion – as ours is doing – is a society that has lost its will to live.

The bombing of abortion clinics

I have two objections to the bombing of abortion clinics. The first is that it is morally wrong. Nobody has the right to take into his or her hands the decision to destroy the property of others. What is being done in the clinics is morally wrong and should be stopped or prevented by the proper authorities.

But for a private individual to decide that this is war and therefore we have the right to destroy the property of the enemy is far beyond the terms of reference of any individual or group which does not have a mandate from the people.

So, I want to state categorically that I not only do not agree with the action but I condemn it in the strongest terms as being unjust and immoral.

Moral ends do not justify immoral means

This age-long principle of moral theology – not just Catholic theology – is still valid. So, not only do I denounce the bombing of clinics or any violence to attain just and praiseworthy ends – even the saving of the lives of unborn babies – I also condemn any immoral action. This includes telling lies.

I have heard and read that there are people in the U.S., very ardent defenders of the unborn, who think it is moral and praiseworthy to phone and say they are pregnant when they are not and even make appointments to have an abortion. The object of this exercise is to confuse the pro-abortionists and make things difficult for them.

I am all for making things difficult for them but within the Commandments of God and lying is against the Eighth Commandment. So, while telling a lie is not in the same category as blowing up a clinic, it is an immoral act and is therefore wrong, even if the end is a worthy one – the saving of the lives of unborn babies.

We must keep our principles right

We, who are called pro-lifers, believe that abortion is wrong because it is the killing of an innocent human being and is therefore against the laws of God. That – as far as I am concerned – is our chief (and, probably, only) reason for taking the stand that we do. But God has more than one law and to break one of His laws in order to defend another cannot be right morally.

I know that this is sometimes difficult to accept but it is a basic truth and to flaunt it is to open the door to all kinds of wrong actions which are prejudicial to any just cause.

My second reason

I said at the beginning that I have two reasons for being against the bombing of abortion clinics – and I nearly forgot the second. It is this.

When people hear and read that a clinic has been bombed or destroyed they tend to lump it all under one heading – it must be those pro-lifers! So, it gives the entire pro-life movement a bad name.

I have been closely connected with the pro-life movement for more than ten years and have attended more meetings than I can count. Never once have I heard it suggested that violence of any kind should be even entertained as an antidote to abortion. Yet, when it is discovered that the perpetrators of the bombings are 'fanatics' or belong to some fanatical group, the tendency remains to look askance at any and every pro-life group and 'just to wonder'.

Picketers

I am all for picketing and – in order to make a point – for civil disobedience, provided it does not involve violence. An excellent example of this was the 'arrest' of some pro-life picketers recently for sitting on the steps outside the Morgentaler Clinic and 'obstructing entrances'.

The point they were making was that the police arrested them for such a minor infringement of the law while babies were being killed inside in defiance not only of the Law of God but of the law of the land.

It's interesting to note that just recently (January 1985) one of the auxiliary bishops of New York, who is black, was arrested for 'obstructing passage' outside the South African Consulate where he was protesting apartheid. In Detroit, the mayor of the city was arrested on the same charge.

Violence is not the answer

So, while I fully support those who brave the weather and give their often-valuable time to picketing outside the abortuary and get arrested for non-violent civil disobedience, I unequivocally condemn any acts or words which break the laws of God. The shocking violence of abortion will never be stopped by the use of another type of violence.

The targets they pick

In its issue of April 28, under the above title, the *Globe and Mail* published a scathing editorial attacking the Pro-Life people who picketed outside the home of one of the doctors who performs abortions at the Morgentaler Clinic. The editorial is characterized by pejorative language and lack of veracity. That the *Globe* should take this position is far from surprising. A perusal of some of its editorials during the late 1960s gives ample proof of the paper's pro-abortion bias.

Blatantly untrue

For instance, the story about two young boys being told to "go knock on her door and tell her to stop killing babies" is simply a distortion of facts. I invite – in fact I challenge – any responsible member of the *Globe and Mail* staff to go to the Campaign Life office and view a video which shows the entire picket. They will see and hear exactly what happened. A national newspaper should be more accurate and honest in its reporting.

The status of the clinic

According to the editorial, the "status of the Morgentaler Clinic, which is not a hospital under the law, remains in limbo." It was doctors Morgentaler and Scott who were charged – not the clinic. At present there are two new doctors performing the abortions.

141

Neither has been charged and both these doctors are breaking the law and being guarded by the 'forces of law and order'. If the Premier of Ontario, the Attorney General of Ontario and the Commissioner of Police were men of their word, both these doctors would have been charged under Section 251 of the Criminal Code. But they are being allowed to continue to murder babies. Dead babies don't have votes!

Character suicide

"Dirty Exercise in Character Assassination!" is how the *Globe and Mail* editorial sums up the peaceful picketing which took place outside Dr. Colodny's house. But in the *Toronto Star* (March 18) Dr. Colodny is quoted as saying, "I'd like people to know that there's a new doctor at the clinic." If a person commits 'character suicide' it is rather difficult to follow it up with 'character assassination'.

The editorial then goes on to take issue with the term 'baby killing' as applied to abortions by the Pro-Life protesters. It states that, "Baby killing is against the law in Canada, whereas the abortion of the 'fetus' is quite legal..." That, of course, is our objection. It is a moral contradiction. According to the findings of genetic science, the difference between a baby in the womb and a baby in its crib is merely one of development. Both have the same right to life which no state can either confer or take away.

I agree

The only part of the editorial with which I agree is the bit which says, "It is far easier to picket a clinic than a major hospital." Of course it is and that's why we do it! It is not because we think that abortions which are performed 'according to the law' in hospi-

142

tals are any less deplorable than those done in the clinic. It is important to make that point clear. The object of picketing or protesting is to make the public aware of something which is wrong. It is much easier to be seen outside a clinic on a residential street than on the crowded thoroughfare outside a large hospital.

The *Globe and Mail* must be aware that two courts in Canada have found, on the facts, that human life begins at conception and that the child is a separate entity from the mother.

Another important reason

But there is another reason for concentrating attention on the "clinic". We have reason to believe that this "clinic" was opened as a 'trial balloon'. If it is accepted by Toronto society – and especially if the government 'looks the other way', similar "clinics" could be started all over the province. Both society and the government have certainly obliged by a mixture of apathy and political expediency. Figuratively speaking, in my opinion, they have as much blood on their hands as the "clinic" staff – and the *Globe and Mail* is running a close third.

Rally

When people asked me how many I expected at the Rally for Life in Toronto on October 1, 1983 I said, "Oh, we should get around fifteen thousand." But, in my heart, I doubted that number and was prepared for a ten thousand total.

Never in my wildest dreams did I – or anybody else for that matter – expect such a tremendous response.

Some say there were forty thousand; the police said there were thirty-five thousand. I'm prepared to settle for anything from twenty-five to thirty thousand. The numbers are important but the spirit is of far greater moment – and spirit there was in abundance! I have tried to analyse it, but somehow it eludes capture. It seemed to be the accumulation of a number of deep emotions.

Perhaps the slow realization, coming to birth, that here is something fearsome – the destruction of human life on a vast scale, the arrogant shaking of the human fist in the face of the Almighty, the donning by puny man of the mantle of God. And all this summed up in the decision by human beings as to which of their brothers and sisters may live or die!

Whether or not my analysis is valid is not important, but whatever knitted that disparate crowd into a close, united body could tax the thinking powers of abler minds and pens than mine.

Joy and Friendship

The atmosphere was one of common joy and mutual friendship – it seemed to ripple through the crowd. People who had never before seen or met each other shook hands and chatted like old friends.

Then came the buses. They rolled up University Avenue like huge tanks and disgorged their human cargo. What a span of humanity that was! Every age and race and occupation of Canada was represented.

Canada in microcosm

I was introduced to an old lady of ninety in a wheel chair and from her down, not a decade was missing: we got the teenagers, the under twelves, the under fives, the infants-in-arms and those who had not yet seen the light of day, and who became the most important people present. In cryptic but trenchant terms, the placards said everything that could be said in favour of the unborn child. The Unborn Babies of Canada were the toast of the occasion.

The power of silence

The silent walk past that sad, sad little building which offers death and destruction to the weak and defenceless was the second most impressive aspect of the day. Speech is silver, silence is golden: thirty thousand people walking in complete silence with heads bowed can speak more eloquently than the writing of a Shakespeare or the oratory of a Churchill. This, I say, was the second most impressive aspect. It was not the apex.

Let them live

That came at the conclusion of the excellent speech

by Chuck Roche, chairman of the Durham Right to Life Association. Chuck was looking for a dramatic ending – was it an inspiration! – he concluded in ringing tones, "Let them live! Let them live!" As if by a sign from the baton of an invisible conductor, the thousands of teenagers in the front lines took up the refrain, "Let them live! Let them live!" It flowed like a huge tidal wave back through the crowd and, within seconds, thirty thousand throats were echoing the cry, "Let them live!"

It was totally spontaneous, and I believe we have found a great expression of the Right to Life. It expresses in three short words everything for which we stand. I challenge the pro-abortionists to take the reverse as their battle cry – "Let them die! Let them die!"

A note of caution

It was a wonderful, exciting and thrilling day; a day etched in our memories forever. But I must sound a note of warning. The war for the unborn is still far from won. On October 1, 1983 we gained a hilltop from which we can survey the scene with renewed hope and courage. But wars have been lost in spite of, and perhaps because of, battles won.

We can never sit back and relax. The 'clinic' is just one small square on a battlefield of immense proportions. Undoubtedly we have gained a few yards, but "We have many miles to go before we sleep."

"People"

Those who are kind enough to read this column may have noticed every now and then I break out in 'people'. I think the reason is that I am temporarily pragmatic. When I come across a complicated machine I do not ask, "How does it work?" but simply, "Does it work?"

While I am convinced that the world needs ideals, I find it difficult to cope with them in the abstract. But when I meet an ideal clothed in flesh and blood and pulsing with life, love and laughter, I find it irresistible. (Now read on!)

Somewhere in New Jersey, U.S., there lives a lady named Jean Garton, Litt. D., L.H.D. She is the wife of a Lutheran clergyman and the mother of four children. She serves on the Lutheran Board of Public Relations and its National Social Concerns Committee. She gave testimony before the U.S. Senate and the House of Representatives on a Human Life Amendment. In 1978 she was numbered among the 'Ten Most Influential Lutherans in the United States'. She is also the author of an excellent book entitled *Who Broke the Baby?* which gives very convincing arguments against abortion in a very readable way. So she does not seem to be your ordinary 'Jane Doe'.

An unwanted pregnancy

In the preface of her book, Jean gives, in capsule

147

form, the story of how she changed from being pro-abortion to being totally pro-life. Her fortieth birthday was approaching, and she was facing it with anticipation. Her three children were at school; bottles and diapers belonged to the past and she had decided to begin an exciting new life. She was going to do all of those things that she had been prevented from doing as a mother with young children. And it was all going to start when the celebrations were over.

Then she discovered that life had begun – but it was not her life. A new life had begun to grow within her. She was pregnant again! She describes it as a very 'unwanted' pregnancy. She was angry and frustrated. It was so unfair. After all those bottles and babies, surely she deserved a break and a little bit of freedom? What about her rights as a woman? She probably even wondered if there was Anyone upstairs!

This was all before the U.S. Supreme Court had given America abortion on demand and, being the wife of a clergyman, she was not going to tangle with the law. So, in her anger, she joined a group which was endeavouring to liberalize the abortion laws.

At the meetings of this group, indoctrination into the language of abortion formed the basis of many of the sessions. The first principle was, "Never accord humanity to what is in the womb". Call it, 'a blob of tissue' or 'the contents of the uterus' or 'the product of conception'. Call it anything you like – as long as you don't call it 'a baby' or 'a child' or anything that would suggest that 'it' is a human being. Stress the 'woman's right to choose' they were told and, at first, Jean lapped this up. But, not only is Jean very intelligent, she is also very sincere and she began to feel increasingly uneasy with these false semantics, which, while being effective and persuasive, lacked integrity.

But she was not going to surrender too easily her objective of widening the scope of the law, so she decided to dig more deeply. She spent many months in study and research on the whole question of unborn life. She read law, medicine and history. She delved into Scripture and the writings of the Church fathers. She says, "I worked long and hard to find evidence to support the theory that the unborn is not human – and found none."

In the end, Jean says she was metaphorically carried kicking and screaming into a pro-life position by the sheer weight of scientific evidence. Language is the agent for change and when language lies, when words are warped and twisted perversely, they are eventually emptied of their true meaning. In the words of Jean Garton, "the linguistic deception of the pro-abortion argument tells it as 'it isn't'."

Jean concludes this part of her story thus, "The unwanted, unplanned pregnancy resulted in a very wanted and loved child. Those who expressed sympathy at my after-forty pregnancy cannot begin to appreciate the special joys and blessings which come to mature mothers. And life did begin at FORTY when I acquired a new and wise teacher in the form of a little boy who taught me what life is really all about."

Jean's book is certainly worth purchasing and reading. It can be obtained by writing to Bethany Fellowship, Inc., 6820 Auto Club Road, Minneapolis, Minnesota 55438.

But if you do get it and read it, don't tell anyone that I filch a lot of my ideas from a book written by the wife of a Lutheran minister!

A man of conviction and action

This September, I had the honour of being the guest speaker at the Edmonton banquet celebrating the tenth anniversary of the foundation of Campaign Life in Alberta. During the evening I was told by quite a few people that I must meet Ken Harcus. I was informed that Ken is a young Baptist teacher, who has taken a very strong and fearless stand against the killing of unborn babies. As a focus he has chosen the Alexandria Hospital in Edmonton. I was introduced to Ken and his story is so interesting and inspiring that I asked him to send me a brief account of the events that led up to his very positive and public action. The remainder of this column is a summary of Ken's account.

Half truths swallowed

Ken says that during his time at university he was fed the usual 'pro-choice' half truths defending abortion. He admits that he swallowed them and was pretty ambivalent about the entire matter. It was really none of his business what women did with or to their kids! But then something happened which hit him like the proverbial 'ton of bricks'.

About four years ago he heard a tragic story of a girl who had been a pupil of his. She had had an abortion and later, apparently in a fit of depression and remorse, she had committed suicide. Not only was Ken stunned, he was galvanized into action. He went to see the Planned Parenthood people and, on questioning them, found that the girl had been given no counselling or help of any kind after the abortion. He went through a period of inner turmoil and felt he had to do 'something'. He had to 'stand up and be counted'. Here is what he did.

Adoption not abortion

Ken purchased an 8 ft. by 8 ft. board and an old van. On the board he printed in large letters these words, "Adoption not abortion. Babies aborted since Christmas – a classroom per day in Alberta..." He chose Christmas as the first day to park the van outside the hospital because, as he says, some 1900 years ago another 'unwanted' baby was born!

He had scarcely begun his campaign when he ran into trouble with the law. In order to put up a public sign, he had to form a company. So, he formed a company with the title, 'Adoption Not Abortion'. That made it legal for him to put up the sign, but there was more to come. There is a bylaw which prohibits the parking of a vehicle more than seventy-two hours in any one spot. So, Ken has to move the van every seventy-two hours to avoid being fined. Then his insurance company refused to insure, because of the danger of the van being damaged by vandals – see later!

Ken usually moves his van from one side of the street to the other at midnight, as it is a very busy street during the daytime. One night he had just moved the van when a police car drew up beside him. He was handed a ticket for 'stunting'. The ticket was for $75. It was a very cold night but Ken had to stand for twenty minutes (at 20 below) because the police would not allow him to get into the car.

He went home and had just got into bed when there was a knock on the door. He went down and was handed a ticket for 'inadequate rear mirrors'. They told him to shovel his sidewalk before morning or he would get another ticket. Who needs enemies with friends like these in the police force!

Vandalism

Here is a list of the things that have been done to Ken's van since he began his witness for the unborn: sprayed with paint twelve times; sign mangled three times; tires slashed and flattened thirty to forty times; headlights, windows and windshield damaged several times; radiator punctured once.

Ken's house was set on fire on November 12, 1984. No suspects were arrested. Ken has received several letters threatening him with dynamiting or kneecapping. The list is not unlike that given by St. Paul in his Letter to the Corinthians (2 Cor. 11). Except that they never smashed St. Paul's headlights!

Rewards

But it has not all been dark. Ken has received letters of congratulation and encouragement. Thousands of people have read the words, "Babies aborted since Christmas – a classroom per day in Alberta". That must help to bring the shocking crime of abortion to the notice of the public. How many babies have been saved from death by Ken's courageous witness?

We shall never know. But there is one of which he is certain. A young man and his pregnant girlfriend had decided that abortion was the 'solution' to their self-made problem. But they saw the sign and the boy realized that Ken had been his former teacher.

152

They visited Ken and he put them in touch with Birthright. They decided against the abortion and a baby girl was born some months afterwards. Ken says that watching the baby play in his living room when they visit him makes everything he has done well worthwhile.

Ken has five children, all very young. He says that they do not yet understand why Daddy's van is always parked outside the hospital. But he knows that a love for life, for other people, and especially for the unborn, will eventually become part of their lives too.

Ken will never know the full fruit of his utterly unselfish sacrifices, nor will he be considered a candidate for a public citation. But his example of Christian love and unwavering faith has inspired many of us who are not blessed with his courage, to do a little more for the defenceless unborn.

Pro-life pilgrimage
to Midland

A pilgrimage is defined as a journey to a sacred spot for religious reasons. Figuratively speaking, pilgrimages have been in existence 'since Adam was a boy'. Muslims travel to Mecca, Buddhists go to Lumbini, where Buddha was born, Sikhs visit various 'gurdward' or temples and Christians visit shrines in many places and countries. I have been on pilgrimages to Jerusalem, Rome, Lourdes and Knock. I have always travelled by land, air or sea – with feet well off the ground. But the pilgrimage to Midland was different. As the African tribe with which I worked translated our expression, 'on foot', we would go 'with feet'. Sounds more accurate to me!

How it all came about

As far as I was personally concerned, this is what happened. One morning I got a phone call from a man named Bob Brookes from Kitchener. He said he would like to come and see me about 'something'. I often get calls like that and I usually try to find out, by judicious questioning, what the 'something' might be. Bob said it was to discuss the forthcoming Pro-Life pilgrimage to Midland. He suggested that it would be a good idea if I became a pilgrim. I expressed interest and enthusiasm until he divulged the fact that we would walk to Midland and it would take five days. I suddenly remembered that I had a lot of engagements during those five days. I couldn't name any of them but I was sure that I was fully committed. After a stony silence on the other end of the line, Bob said that he would come to see me all the same.

No escape

Bob Brookes is one of those people who not only 'enthuse' you but 'infuse' you. I admitted that whatever vague engagements I had could be changed. By the time he had expostulated on the benefits to me personally – both spiritual and physical – and to the whole Pro-Life Movement I felt like a horse champing at the bit and pawing the ground. But when he got down to specifics, my ardour began to cool. "Do you have a sleeping bag, Father?" "No, Bob. I always sleep either in bed or at my office desk. It's at least thirty years since I slept in a bag." "Well, it's high time you started again. Do you have walking shoes, Father?" "No, Bob, I don't walk. I always drive." "That's why you look the way you do. You need a lot of exercise. Are you a good cook, Father?" "No, Bob. I can just about make a cup of tea if somebody boils the water and hands me a tea bag." "That's all right. We'll see that you don't starve. Just keep your collar on and look hungry and somebody will feed you. We'll need you for saying Mass so we'll keep you half alive!" There was no escaping. Every time I tried to make an excuse he eyed me with the gaze of a predatory hawk about to swoop on a helpless sparrow. His glance seemed to say, "You're not the man we thought you were." And so I was committed – at least to some extent!

The sleeping bag

The first thing I had to do was get a sleeping bag. Dan McCash said he had a lovely one. I called round and Dan produced the bag from the basement. It was bright red. Dan remarked that sleeping in this bag would be the nearest I would ever get to being a Monsignor. He then went into a scientific explanation of how the bag worked. You didn't need to wear anything when you slept in the McCash bag. The combination of your 'natural body heat' and the stuffing which lined the bag made the climate just perfect. In fact Dan suggested that I would be so comfortable that I might even lose some marks 'Up Above'. But of that later!

The pilgrimage in action

The pilgrimage started from different points on Sunday, August 10th. I was doing a ministry at Streetsville on that day. On Monday I drove from Streetsville to meet the pilgrims at Orangeville. They had slept in a garden behind a restaurant. I celebrated Mass for them and after breakfast they began walking to the Cistercian Monastery, miles from there. I drove as I couldn't carry the car. Needless to say I got there hours before they did; so I decided to do some praying, eating and sleeping. The hardships of the pilgrimage were beginning to tell on me! That night the pilgrims slept in the open – not in a monastery garden but in a monastery field. I slept very comfortably in the barn – the horse was on holidays! We arose early in the morning and attended the Office and Mass in the Monastery Chapel. It was really beautiful to hear the Divine Office recited with such reverence – with 'unhurried pace', followed by concelebrated Mass of equal devotion. It set the mood for the day. I sneaked into the visitors' dining room and had eggs for breakfast, while the 'common folk' lit their camp fires and boiled their pots of all kinds of beverages and messes of various varieties of curds and whey and porridges.

Bob always had a solution

But what was I to do with the car? Bob had the
answer. His very attractive daughter Tracey with friend
of similar ilk named Shirley, was to drive a van with
all the luggage – tents, sleeping bags, food boxes,
etc., to the next stopping place where we were to
spend the night. It was a park somewhere near Barrie.
I would follow them in my car, leave it there, drive
back with them in the van and then proceed to 'hoof
it' with the pilgrims. The nearest I have come to being
a marathon runner in the past twenty years might be
summed up as follows: Walk from home to car, enter
car, drive to office, alight from car, climb five steps,
enter office and sit down at desk. This procedure is
reversed at 5 p.m. sharp each afternoon. This will
give the reader some idea of how 'fit' I am for a
twenty mile or so hike per day on a dusty road in
the August heat. But it is amazing how the human
frame can adapt to varying circumstances. With the
singing of rather jaunty hymns, the reciting of rosaries
and the telling of jokes, I was soon into the swing
of things and was tempted at times to break into, "It's
a long way to Tipperary". Looking at some of the
pilgrims who were even older than I am I felt
ashamed. They had walked for two days and refused
to ride in the vans which kept along with us in case
of accidents or illness. Now and then, when the going
got tough and the tough got going, I bent down to
tie my lace and slipped into the rear van and snoozed
for an hour or so.

The camp

I don't know how many miles I walked – but it was
less than everybody else. By now I had no doubt
about the fact that we were doing the pilgrimage 'with

feet'. I had never before been so conscious of the fact that my body ends 'with feet'. They were sore, a little swollen and very tired. When we eventually arrived at the park, everything was there because the girls had unloaded the van in the morning. Tents were erected and fires lighted and tea and coffee were brewed in a very short time. There were more types and sizes of stove than I had ever seen. it all looked 'like an army set in battle array'. Everybody had food except me. So, following Bob's instructions, I donned my collar and began walking around greeting everyone and being fed like a stray dog. By the time I had visited four or five tents I was fully 'fed and watered'. I made a mental note of the people who had staved off my hunger so that I would not visit them for breakfast! Then news came that there was a lake and a swimming pool and showers about a mile away. The crowd took off like a bunch of bats out of Hell. I followed, not 'with feet' but 'with wheels' and after a shower I began to feel human again.

The camp fire

By the time I got back to our base, a camp fire was blazing and people were sitting around it singing. We spent an hour or so, chanting, telling jokes and laughing. Then at about 10 p.m. Father Bill Truze, a wonderful young priest who is the chief inspiration of the pilgrimage, clapped his hands for silence. We said evening prayer together, sang a hymn and went in the direction of our tents.

If you have tears – prepare to shed them next month when I continue this epic. Under the heading 'A Night to Remember' I shall relate the story of my first experience in thirty years, 'Awake in a sleeping bag'.

158

Pro-life pilgrimage to Midland – Part II

Father Bill and I were sharing a tent but he was having a meeting with some of the organizers to plan for tomorrow. So I slipped quietly into our tent to get ready for 'bed'. It was quite dark but I found the red sleeping bag and unzipped it. It was very cold by this time so I decided to keep on all my clothes, except my shoes until heat was generated by what Dan described as my 'body heat'.

I got my feet in and then the rest of me and tried to zip myself up. The zip was on the outside and my hands were inside but I got it up as far as my neck and decided to settle for that until Father Bill would arrive and complete the interment. I lay on my back counting the bones in my spine and feeling like a cross between a sardine and an Egyptian mummy.

I must have dropped off to sleep immediately from sheer fatigue. But at some hour of the night I wakened. I had no idea what time it was as the darkness was nothing less than 'Stygian'. I didn't have a luminous watch and I had no flashlight. But that was not the worst. I was simply freezing. Either nature had forgotten to turn on my 'body heat' system or Dan's marvellous sleeping bag was lined with the wrong stuff.

Father Bill was 'sawing wood' for all he was worth and somebody in an adjoining tent was replying in kind. I was still lying on my back and I decided to

159

turn. But it was something like attempting to turn a large trailer in Yonge Street during lunch hour. It was just impossible. I was convinced that I had at least triple pneumonia and I did not expect to last till morning.

I hadn't the heart to wake Father Bill who, I knew, had walked for the past two days and must have been worn out. So I decided to depend on whatever credit was left on my 'Spiritual Master Card' and die quietly without the ministrations of a priest.

Dawn

I must have dropped off asleep again for I wakened to see some light stealing through the flap of the tent and was astonished to find that I was still alive – and well! The cold was still there but the freeze had gone. I struggled out of the bag and crept out on hands and knees. My car was about a hundred yards away so I got in to read my breviary. It was cold so I started the engine and let it turn over quietly as the camp was still asleep.

Very soon I began to snooze but suddenly remembered that people can die in running cars if they leave the windows closed – which I had done. I don't know how long it takes to die in those circumstances, but it was a good half-hour before anybody appeared in the camp. This was my second close brush with death in twenty-four hours.

The Poles

We celebrated Mass at about 7 a.m. Then breakfast and on the road again. This day was pretty much like the one before – walking, praying, singing, laughing. But the evening was very different. A Polish pilgrimage had left Toronto a few days before we did and by arrangement we were to meet at a certain spot – a lovely farm graciously loaned by the farmer and his wife. We got there first, around six in the evening. Then we heard singing from far away. Soon it got nearer and we saw the Poles – over one hundred of them – marching in step and looking much fresher than we did. We welcomed them with open arms and it was a really emotional moment. Then fires were lighted and the aroma of the very varied menus floated on the breeze.

I did the 'stray dog' trick again and devoured everything from English ham to Polish sausage. After dinner a huge camp fire was lighted and we sat around it and sang. The Polish contingent entertained us with their beautiful songs full of pathos. It reminded me of what G.K. Chesterton said about the Irish, "Their wars are always merry; their songs are always sad."

At ten sharp, Father Bill clapped his hands and we said evening prayer and everybody went to tent. I didn't even take off my shoes but I can't remember anything else, or whether Dan's bag worked or not. I just lay down and slept till the sun rose on another day.

Farewell

I had to part with them that morning. I had a wedding rehearsal in the afternoon. I got somebody to drive my car the few miles to the crossroads where I would turn off and walked with the crowd. When we got to where the road turned for Barrie and Toronto, we stopped and had a farewell celebration.

I was feted as if I had led the army instead of skulking along behind snatching illegal bouts of slumber and eating everybody else's food. The laity

161

really spoil us priests! After I had given them my blessing, they cheered as if I had just scored the winning goal in the Stanley Cup. As I slowly moved away, I had some difficulty in driving for my eyes were filled with tears.

People are really wonderful!

Silent night

I think I celebrated about twenty-six Christmases in Kenya, East Africa. But the only one that stands out in my memory is the first.

It was 1942 and in those days there were no distractions such as television and radio out in the 'bush' so Midnight Mass was one of the big events of the year. Everybody came to it – Catholics, Protestants, pagans. Night falls early in Africa and it was pitch dark by 9 p.m.

A heart-stirring sight

The pastor (long since dead) suggested to me that I should go out and watch the people coming down the hills. I said, "But I won't be able to see them." He replied, "Go and see."

I went out and a strangely heart-moving sight met my eyes. The hills were alive with small dots of light – swaying and moving. Each family brought their own little oil lamp as there were no lights in the church.

Some people walked more than thirty miles and would return home after Mass. As they arrived in the compound, there were introductions and greetings interspersed with laughter.

Alive with a 'joy'

Some had not met since the previous Christmas, others

for perhaps a few years and then there were the many who came for the first time. The whole night was alive with a 'Joy' which this world alone cannot give.

Bethlehem all over again

It was a long wait until 11 p.m. when the church would open. But it is a warm time of the year so they sat in groups on the grass and chatted. Then the young people began to dance their own native dances, while the old talked about 'better times' and 'days long gone'.

A donkey carrying a young, pregnant woman and led by a tired man would have blended perfectly into the scene. And perhaps there would have been 'room'.

Church packed

At 11 p.m. the bell sounded, the doors opened and the people crowded into the church. It was quite a large building but it was filled to overflowing. There were no fire regulations in those days and the lighted lamps constituted a fire hazard. But nobody even thought of such a thing as they silently took their places along the low seats. Apart from the crying of the multitudes of babies, there was no other sound in the church.

Carols and tears

Before Mass began, the children's choir sang carols. I sat in the sanctuary and listened – enthralled. When they sang *Silent Night* in the Kikuyu language, my heart overflowed through my eyes and memories flooded back.

Christmas, celebrated in a different culture and expressed in what was then for me a strange tongue,

164

stirs the soul at such a deep level that the experience cannot be rendered captive in the bonds of mere human words.

At the end of Mass the people came to see the crib. I sat at the side and watched their faces in the dim light of the lanterns. What impressed me most was the expression on the faces of the pagan women, with their own babies at their breasts, as they looked with wonder at the Child and His Mother.

Motherhood in 'pagan' Africa is a woman's greatest glory and the story of a maiden who became pregnant with the Son of God, though they could but vaguely grasp its significance, elevated the entire concept of pregnancy to a level far beyond the bounds of human understanding.

Different meanings of Christmas

After Mass, we stood outside the church greeting the people as they started back on what was, for some, several hours walk through the bush. But they were happy and, as the voices faded, that mystical silence of the African night enveloped us again.

Father Lynch turned to me and said, "For the African, Christmas is over." For the white man, it had scarcely begun.

The Rosary

As a devotion and a prayer, the Rosary has been beloved by widely differing categories and social groups wtihin the Catholic Church over a period of more than five hundred years. It is the prayer of saints and of sinners and it is the form of extra-liturgical prayer most frequently recommended by popes from Leo XIII to John Paul II.

How the Rosary developed

The Rosary was not a 'one-shot deal.' Nobody sat down and thought it out as one might formulate a plan of action. No, it developed slowly over many years. In the early years of the Church the monks began praying the 150 psalms in common. The laity wished to be part of this prayer of the Church but very few could read. So, they were given beads and taught to pray 150 Pater Nosters (Our Fathers). The monks used to read extracts from the Scriptures between the praying of the psalms, so the faithful began to interlace 'events' from the Gospels – repeated from memory – between the praying of the Our Fathers. This helped to make the prayer more interesting and less monotonous.

The Dominicans

The Dominican Fathers – an order of preachers founded by St. Dominic in the year 1215 A.D., – were the most ardent in spreading devotion to the

166

Rosary. I think they were chiefly responsible for the form of the Rosary as we know it today. They divided the events or mysteries into three groups, the Joyful Mysteries, the Sorrowful Mysteries and the Glorious Mysteries. The joyful events remind us of the early life of Christ; the sorrowful remind us of the Passion of Christ and the glorious remind us of the events which took place after the death of Christ. So the Rosary is a completely 'Biblical Prayer' as will be obvious from a brief description of how we pray it. The introduction consists of the Apostles Creed, one Our Father and three Hail Marys – in honour of the Blessed Trinity. The events or mysteries follow. On Mondays and Thursdays the Joyful Events are recalled and each one is followed by reciting one Our Father, ten Hail Marys and one Glory be to the Father.

The joyful mysteries

The first Joyful Mystery is the Annunciation, which reminds us of the Angel Gabriel being sent to 'announce' to the Virgin Mary that she was to be the Mother of the Saviour. This is found in the Gospel of St. Luke, Chap. 1, vv26-38. The second event is the Visitation, Luke 1, vv39-56 – which recalls the beautiful episode in which Mary makes the long journey of some ninety miles from Nazareth to El Karim to help her cousin Elizabeth, who was carrying John the Baptist in her womb. This is surely the event which the pro-life people could claim as their own. For it was then that one unborn baby recognized Another and leaped for joy in his mother's womb. The third event commemorated is the Birth of Jesus at Bethlehem – the most famous Birth in history! The fourth event is the Presentation in the Temple and the fifth, the Finding in the Temple. If you read the early chapters of the Gospel of St. Luke you will find very little that is not recalled in the Joyful Mysteries of the Rosary.

The sufferings of Christ

The second group of events is named 'The Sorrowful Mysteries.' They are found in all four Gospels in various detail. They are first, The Agony in the Garden; second, The Scourging at the Pillar; third, The Crowning with Thorns; fourth, The Carrying of the Cross; fifth, The Crucifixion and Death. Read the story of the Passion of Christ in any or all the Gospels and you will find that it is all summed up in the Sorrowful Mysteries of the Rosary. So when we pray these mysteries or events on Tuesdays and Fridays we mentally review the story of our redemption.

The glorious mysteries

The Glorious Events, recited on Sundays, Wednesdays and Saturdays, are a quick 'flash-back' to the wonderful happenings which followed the death of Christ – the most famous death in history. The first event mentioned is, of course, His resurrection – recorded in all four Gospels, referred to in the Acts of the Apostles, the First Letter of St. Peter and in almost every one of the Letters of St. Paul – "If Christ be not risen, then our preaching is in vain." The second event is the Ascension of Christ of which we read in the Gospels of Sts. Matthew, Mark and Luke. The most detailed description is found in the Acts, Chap. I, vv 6-11. The third Glorious Event is the Descent of the Holy Spirit at Pentecost. This is the event which, as it were, put God the Father's seal on the entire life of Christ. The two final events are the Assumption of Mary into Heaven and her crowning as Queen of Heaven. These events are not found directly in Scripture, but are taken from the Tradition of the early Church and the belief of Catholics throughout the ages.

The Gospel in miniature

The Rosary is usually thought of as a prayer to Mary. But really it is not. It is an inspired summary of the entire Gospel story of most of which, from the birth at Bethlehem to the last breath on Calvary, Mary was the chief witness. The Rosary has sometimes been called a 'senseless repetition'. But a little reflection will tell us that it is basic psychology. It is only in the fairly recent past that society has discovered the psychological power of constant repetition. Modern advertising is founded on this basic principle that if something is repeated often enough it will make an impact. Corporations spend millions of dollars every year repeating a name or an idea on radio and TV. So it must work! Why should we not use this same principle of repetition to instil into our hearts and minds and those of our children the salient points of the Greatest Story Ever Told? The daily reminder that God loves us so much that He sent His Son to redeem us can and should keep our values right and help us to put the things of this world in proper perspective.

Yes, I'm a radical

A few months ago, when visiting Edmonton, I was interviewd by a young lady from the *Western Catholic Reporter*. She plied me with the usual questions about my background and my involvement with the Pro-Life Movement. Then she shot this question at me, "How do you feel about being considered a radical?"

Like a seasoned rugby player, I side-stepped the question by saying, "Most people who call us radicals do absolutely nothing themselves. It is merely a cop-out." She accepted this and went on to something else.

What is a radical?

Next morning I was trying to pray in a church and the question came back to me, "Am I a radical?" I looked up at the stark wooden crucifix above the altar and began to think almost aloud.

The word 'radical' comes from the Latin 'radix' meaning 'a root'. It means getting below the surface of things and down to the foundation. Sometimes the opposite of a word can bring out its significance better than the word itself. The opposite of radical is 'superficial', which means 'above the face' or on the surface. Perhaps the adjective 'shallow' could best describe a superficial person. I don't mind being called 'stupid' or 'dumb' or 'ugly', but I would hate to be considered shallow.

Christ the radical

I looked back at the crucifix. There is something awfully radical about nailed hands, fettered feet, a thorn-crowned head and a riven side. It occurred to me that Christ must be the original radical. I began to look for a simpler term for radical than 'radical', and my natural built-in computer came up with the expression, 'no compromise'.

Yes, I think that's it. To be radical means that a person will not compromise on certain fundamental principles.

Applying this to my own life, I realized that there are certain things on which I am prepared to compromise and certain things on which I would never compromise – even in the face of death.

For instance, I am not prepared to die in defence of having my eggs scrambled rather than fried for breakfast. Neither would I take a life-or-death stand on which highway somebody uses to drive me home – provided I get home! These matters are on the surface and to be inflexible about them is to be immature, unreasonable and foolish.

Fundamental principles

But there are principles or truths on which, I hope, I would never compromise. I say 'hope' because, through human weakness I might do 'a Simon Peter' and say "I know not the Man." But my present mind set is such that I hope I would sacrifice even life itself rather than compromise certain truths which form the basis of my whole outlook on life.

If asked to mention just a few, I would probably choose the existence of God, the divinity of Christ and my loyalty to the Church. These truths, and many others which are based on them, are so deeply rooted and embedded in my soul that to compromise on any one of them would mean being totally untrue to myself.

Logical consequences

But if I am radical about these truths, I cannot be less radical about the logical consequences that flow from them. If I am radical about two plus two equalling four, I cannot be less radical about the fact that forty-four plus forty-four equals eighty-eight.

If I believe that "God is the Sovereign Lord of Heaven and earth and of all things," I must just as firmly believe that He is total Master of life and death and, therefore, without His permission, nobody can decide who will live and who will die.

Based on the findings of science and the statements of scientists, I am convinced that the unborn baby is a true human being from the moment of conception. Therefore, I must be radical about the right of every unborn baby to be born and to be given all the care it needs to survive. To deny this truth or to refuse to defend it, would be tantamount, in my opinion, to denying the lordship of God over life and death.

We need radicals

So I am grateful to the reporter of the *Western Catholic Reporter*. She made me face up to myself. I shall never again dodge or side-step the question, "Are you a radical?"

My answer will be, "Yes, I am a radical on the truths which I consider fundamental – and the right to life of every unborn baby is one of those truths."

172

One of the many problems with our current society is this. We have allowed the principle of democracy – valid in certain circumstances – to so pervade our lives that we have ceased to think for ourselves and so we walk with the crowd. What we have forgotten is the fact that if something is morally wrong, it remains morally wrong – even if one hundred per cent of people say it is morally right or vice versa.

Here is a verse which expresses better than I can what I have been trying to say. "Some men die by the sword and others go down in flames. But most men perish inch by inch in play and little games."

God preserve me from such a fate. Register me as a Radical!